Future-proof Your Legal Career

10 Core Areas of Professional Development

Clare Jones
Steve Couch
Hannah Beko

Globe Law and Business

Authors
Clare Jones, Steve Couch and Hannah Beko

Managing director
Sian O'Neill

Future-proof Your Legal Career: 10 Core Areas of Professional Development
is published by

Globe Law and Business Ltd
3 Mylor Close
Horsell
Woking
Surrey GU21 4DD
United Kingdom
Tel: +44 20 3745 4770
www.globelawandbusiness.com

Printed and bound by Severn, Gloucester, UK

Future-proof Your Legal Career: 10 Core Areas of Professional Development

ISBN 9781787424265
EPUB ISBN 9781787424272
Adobe PDF ISBN 9781787424289

Table of contents

Foreword

Sarah Goulbourne
gunner*cooke*

As a founder of one of the UK's most innovative and fastest-growing 'challenger' law firms and a former practising lawyer, I've met and worked with many lawyers. During my 30 years as a lawyer and qualified coach working in a range of businesses, I have often been struck by the fact that career guidance and coaching for lawyers can be lacking. This book aims to fill some of that gap.

In my coaching work, I often find myself surprised by how many of my peers can feel overwhelmed by their legal career and become anxious about their future. This is understandable. Lawyers of the 2020s operate in a ferociously competitive arena and face unprecedented complexity and pace of change. Competing demands to be all things, including a technical expert, efficient manager and 'rainmaker', can be exhausting. Meanwhile, many firms have had to reimagine their entire operations and staffing, which has led to even more uncertainty. Numerous challenges abound from the post-pandemic climate; clients demanding 'more for less'; rapid regulatory and legislative changes; technological advances; and competing market entrants with innovative new business models.

Our hyper-connected world presents a pace of change that requires contemporary lawyers to stretch continually and perhaps even reinvent themselves as they advance. Professional development skills are critical. It is time to take charge of your career as a core competitive strategy for robust future practice and personal wellbeing.

To me, the best lawyers understand **goals**, both their own and those of their clients. They have **charisma**; they're **commercial** and **innovative**; they are good at **relationships** and **winning** work; they work well in **teams** as **leaders** and **collaborators**. They also have good **ideas** and embrace **change**. These skills and attributes are perennial, despite our world of disruption and are discussed in this book.

Through stories and examples, case studies, interviews, tips, checklists, exercises and assignments, the authors aim to foster your growth and nurture your dreams. You are invited to create your own dynamic personal development programme and hold yourself accountable for delivering it.

This book is written for private practice lawyers primarily at the mid to senior level. However, early-career and in-house lawyers may also gain valuable insights. Applying some of the ideas presented in this book will position any lawyer to contribute more meaningfully to the world and shape a brilliant future career.

Lead author Clare Jones and co-authors Steve Couch and Hannah Beko are coaches, all of whom I've worked with closely, rate highly and recommend. Each of them has drawn on their deep and extensive professional knowledge to help you reflect on and plan how you want your legal career to develop. They each bring different coaching styles and philosophies, presenting you with a wide range of approaches and viewpoints.

Clare Jones is chief marketing officer at TLT LLP, where she is responsible for business development, marketing and knowledge strategy. In her 25 years as a chartered marketer working in global firms and digital agencies, she has delivered innovative, international, multi-channel campaigns, generated leads and won work. As a coach, she has helped hundreds of lawyers to build their personal brands, engage with the market and delight clients.

Steve Couch is a former 'Big 4' tax partner with over 30 years of experience, which included six years of leading practices across Europe advising multinational clients on cross-border legal issues. In 2019 he completed an MSc in Coaching & Behavioural Change (with distinction) from Henley Business School. He leads his coaching practice, *Coaching Together*. His work includes coaching partners, senior staff and leadership teams in professional service practices, researching, writing and presenting.

Hannah Beko is a highly experienced commercial property lawyer. Alongside her legal practice, Hannah leads her training and coaching consultancy, *Authentically Speaking*, supporting law firms, individual lawyers and legal business owners in their development of key professional skills including stress management, improving emotional well-being, effective leadership and business growth and development.

Every chapter of this book provides excellent and thought-provoking questioning to prompt your growth through self-reflection. Good coaching questions, the DNA of excellent coaching, can give you, as a busy, competent lawyer, the space to step back and examine your thinking and actions. The right question can stop you in your tracks; it can make you think hard and intensely and see yourself from a different perspective or help you begin to imagine new solutions to existing challenges.

Instead of hiring a great coach, which is always a good idea, the goal with this book is that you begin working on your career by coaching yourself. Hence the plethora of questions provided. After all, you know best what is right for you. While there are many coaching questions you can't prepare for in advance, it's about being ready to look at yourself truthfully and being open to exploring new ways of thinking, being and acting. Fundamentally, it's all about your intent. I suggest you get yourself into a coaching mindset, where you build your awareness, are prepared to dig deep and focus your thinking on your vast potential *before* you even begin to read this book.

Of course, we'd love you to have a brilliant coach by your side who could, in particular, help you with accountability and actions towards your goals, but we also recognise that this is not always feasible. If you have a coach or intend to work with one, this book can become a valuable companion.

The book's 10 chapters draw on a range of exciting contributions from experts and present an overview of the best contemporary research to trigger new insights for you on future-proofing your legal career.

In Chapter I, Hannah explores your dreams for your future career and how to create plans for achieving those goals.

In Chapter II, Clare explores 'charisma' and its value to your legal career; she interviews Charlie Geffen, chair of the International Stock Exchange Group, and considers how you can craft a strategy to help you build a sustainable reputation.

Hannah looks at what it means to be commercial as a lawyer in Chapter III. She hears from a dynamic corporate lawyer, Dr Michelle Chen, about what clients want to see.

Hannah then examines innovation in the legal profession in Chapter IV. She considers what this means for lawyers and law firms and how they can further their careers by identifying more innovative opportunities in their practice.

In Chapter V, Steve looks at relationships, building more awareness of the clients you service, and cultivating advanced interpersonal skills, particularly a growth mindset.

Clare then looks at how you can master quotes, bids, pitches and proposals in Chapter VI and interviews David Abbott, an international pricing expert, for unusual tips on pricing to win.

Steve reviews contemporary leadership in Chapter VII, looking at approaches and their underlying influences. He hears from Vikki Leach, founder and principal consultant at Inclusion Consulting Ltd who looks at measuring personal leadership effectiveness and preparing for future leadership challenges.

During Chapter VIII, Steve then examines different aspects of working in teams where increasing complexity requires more frequent collaboration to address client needs.

Clare discusses sharing ideas and how to build your reputation in Chapter IX. She speaks to Chris Rushworth, business development and marketing director at TLT LLP, on 'thought leadership' and then interviews Rosie Burbidge, prolific ideas sharer and intellectual property law partner at gunner*cooke* LLP.

Finally, in Chapter X, Clare discusses the ubiquitous topic of change. She speaks to Chris Georgiou, partner and head of Ashurst ADVANCE, on what Ashurst lawyers are doing to manage change and what you might need to consider next.

Indeed, the only certainty we have in life is change. You can create tremendous change from within. A decision to change takes a second. I believe everyone can learn, grow and change. The impacts can be profoundly empowering and joyful.

I know you want to be successful, but you have to embrace your development. Ongoing personal and professional development is an integral part of every successful career. I do believe that you can do and be anything you want and that the work towards this has to come from you. Reading this book may well be the catalyst you've been seeking, and I am proud of and excited by the ideas presented to help you on your journey.

> *We but mirror the world. All the tendencies present in the outer world are to be found in the world of our body. If we could change ourselves, the tendencies in the world would also change. As a man changes his own nature, so does the attitude of the world change towards him. This is the divine mystery supreme. A wonderful thing it is and the source of our happiness. We need not wait to see what others do.*
> Mahatma Gandhi[1]

I'd love you to use this book as a reference guide to help you build a sustainable, rewarding legal career. The 10 core areas we discuss are enduring aspects of your professional development. Why not keep this book on your bookshelf at eye level or as part of your essential toolkit for you to dip into and maybe try something new?

Good luck on your journey, and don't forget to enjoy what lies ahead.

1 www.goodreads.com/quotes/760902-we-but-mirror-the-world-all-the-tendencies-present-in.

Chapter I:

Know yourself and your goals

Hannah Beko

This introductory chapter will explore your dreams and aspirations for your future career and create some rock-solid plans for achieving those goals. What is it that you want for yourself, your life and your career? How can you make a road map to reach your goals? How can you deal with blocks and challenges?

> *A goal without a plan is just a wish.*
> Antoine de Saint-Exupéry[1]

> *Setting goals is the first step of turning the invisible into the visible.*
> Tony Robbins[2]

1. Who sets your goals?

There has been a problem with traditional goal setting we are familiar with in the corporate world of law. Our goals, particularly our career goals, are often set by our organisation or our boss and are presented to us as something that we have to achieve in the next 12 months. The annual review traditionally consists of a list of priorities for the

1 www.goodreads.com/quotes/87476-a-goal-without-a-plan-is-just-a-wish.
2 www.brainyquote.com/quotes/tony_robbins_147791.

coming year and a re-setting of KPIs based on an increase from the previous year.

It's been done this way for a long time, but does it work?

Where we don't have ownership of our own goals, where they haven't come from ourselves and what we want, we aren't particularly attached to them. Because of this, it can be tough for us to achieve them as we do not feel invested on a personal level. It may not be enjoyable or a way that makes us feel that we're growing as a person. It's not to say that goals won't be reached but attaining them comes from fear of letting others down or not achieving the standards expected by your firm and what implications that may have in the future. It is a negative motivator in that we are looking to get away from what we don't want to feel or experience, rather than moving positively towards something we do want.

In *Taming Tigers*, Jim Lawless talks about the importance of being positively motivated towards your goals, rather than being in fear of what might happen if you didn't achieve them. "Once you are motivated 'towards', you have power. Immense power. Now you have the ability to bring your whole self – mind, body and spirit – to the activity."[3] Imagine how much easier achievements might become!

1.1 Is your career already mapped out for you?

The legal profession is very good at mapping out a career path for us all the way from degree to law school, to training contract and then the various stages of our post-qualification career up to partnership level. Whilst at the time of writing changes are envisaged to the traditional path of qualification, these are perhaps unlikely to alter the expected trajectory for most solicitors.

It is easy to get on the treadmill or conveyor belt and see those as the natural goals or automatic steps ahead of you. How often do lawyers stop to ask if those goals are meaningful for them, if it is something that they

3 Jim Lawless, *Taming Tigers: Do Things You Never Thought You Could*, Virgin Books, 2012, p88.

want to achieve, or if at certain times in their lives, those milestones are the right ones for them?

1.2 Are you at risk of drifting?

Drift is the enemy of an intentional life. It happens when we conform to society, don't design our life or future, and just do the things we think we are supposed to do without giving them much thought.[4]

In the legal profession we spend our early years throughout education and training being focused and intentional, but once we end up in our careers this purpose seems to go out the window and is replaced by hard work and more hard work!

CASE STUDY – SAMUEL

As an eight-year qualified lawyer, Samuel had worked for some of the largest firms in the world as he proudly told me. Now looking for his next position, considering his future, perhaps starting a family, he had made an automatic assumption that his future would be with another large prestigious firm. After some exploration through his coaching sessions about what he really wanted from his career, his life and his future, he realised that the sorts of firms he was looking at would very likely be incompatible with the life he wanted to create. It was time to choose between the firm and the life he saw for himself.

A very wise man once said the law is "a great career, but a terrible job".[5] We can thank Philip Jepson, a lawyer turned legal recruiter for this

4 Andy Storch, *Own Your Career Own Your Life*, Andy Storch Inc, 2020, p148.

5 Philip Jepson, "Taking control of your legal career", Jepson Holt Legal Search & Recruitment, p9, https://jepsonholt.com/wp-content/uploads/2020/05/Taking-control-of-your-legal-career_compressed.pdf.

pearl of wisdom. If we drift along in a career like this, without focus and intention, without being clear about what we want, we not only will not achieve what we're capable of, but it will feel like a long, hard slog to boot.

2. What is the best way to set goals?

A different, and perhaps more creative approach, is to spend time thinking about what it is that we really want on a personal and individual level. This might be in our careers, or in our personal life, or in relation to our health or our finances. Frequently we may have aspirations for improvement in all of these areas. Whatever area it is for you at present, it is essential to set aside some time on a reasonably regular basis to think about what it is that you want.

Before defining your goals, it can be helpful to start thinking about your 'big vision'. This is a broader definition of what it is that you want from your career and life. Goals tend to be, by their very nature, quite specific, which we will come on to later. A vision is much broader.

> *Vision is a destination – a fixed point to which we focus all effort. Strategy is a route – an adaptable path to get us where we want to go.*
> Simon Sinek[6]

> *One's vision is not a road map but a compass.*
> Peter Block[7]

2.1 What does 'success' mean to you?

Before you start writing down your goals, it's essential to consider the long-term picture for you. The handy conveyor belt set out by the profession should not be used to measure success or become an automatically adopted road map. What is your version of success, something that is personal to you? It is too easy to say, 'I want to be a partner because that's seen as the pinnacle of the career'.

6 Twitter, 13 August 2012, https://twitter.com/simonsinek/status/235068415075840000?lang=en.
7 www.azquotes.com/quote/667314.

CASE STUDY – RICHARD

Richard moved firms following the promise of partnership. He worked his way through the firm requirements and reached that 'coveted' status. He brought in new clients, built a team and increased revenues. But he found that the weight of the title 'partner' (pressure not from his firm but that he put on himself) was something he didn't want in life, and he moved on elsewhere, shedding the partner title. If you were to ask him now (as many recruiters do) if he would like a partnership title again, he will say no every time. It's no longer a part of his vision or a measure of success in his life.

In *Own Your Career Own Your Life* Andy Storch says: "Unless you are signing a contract to join the military or law firm as a partner, you can almost always change your mind later."[8] But, even as a partner in a law firm, you can (and if it's right you should) change your mind with the appropriate notice and arrangements.

This is my favourite definition of success:

> *Success is liking yourself, liking what you do, and liking how you do it.*
>
> Maya Angelou[9]

If we adopt this version of success, rather than the one that is typically laid out before us in our profession, then we can start to think about what it is that makes us happy, what we enjoy, the best way that we find to work and how we can put all those elements together and think about a plan for our future.

8 Andy Storch, *Own Your Career Own Your Life*, Andy Storch Inc, 2020, www.linkedin.com/pulse/owning-your-career-starts-vision-andy-storch/?articleId=6630110298219048961.

9 www.goodreads.com/quotes/1208-success-is-liking-yourself-liking-what-you-do-and-liking.

2.2 Why do you need a vision?

Marianne Page, the author of *Simple, Logical, Repeatable,* explains a lack of vision very clearly. Without a clear idea of where we're heading in our life and career, it's like getting into the car without a map or (more likely these days) a satellite navigation system. We can drive around for hours, but not get anywhere. Fine for a Sunday drive, but not for our whole lives. "Knowing your destination is crucial. It keeps you focused. It inspires your team. It gives purpose and meaning to your planning."[10]

The goals we set are the strategy, the route or the road map. The vision is the compass or the destination. For this reason, a vision can be abstract or perhaps even vague, it can be a feeling rather than a defined picture.

Your vision can be what you see in your future when you allow yourself to dream:

- What do you want to see yourself doing?
- How do you want to feel about the various aspects of your life?
- Do you want to spend more time doing a certain activity, or perhaps less time doing it?

Most importantly it's about how you want to feel and how you see yourself. Once you have done some work on creating the bigger picture, the vision, the goals or milestones become easier to define.

CASE STUDY – GEMMA

I met Gemma just after she'd finished her training contract. She had been unemployed for a few months and was feeling deflated and unsure about her next steps. I remember, however, that she was very clear about what it was she wanted in the future, a role in international commercial litigation. She held on to this 'dream' and

10 Marianne Page, *Simple, Logical, Repeatable*, Rethink Press Ltd, 2017, p62.

just over two years later secured a position at a new up-and-coming firm doing exactly the work she wanted to be doing. We don't always need to know the 'how', it's enough to hold the vision and we will naturally make the decisions which take us closer to what we want. That's the power of a vision, a compass to your destination.

2.3 What is visualisation?

Visualisation is a powerful tool used in the sports industry. Encyclopedia.com says:

> *Visualization in sport is a training technique that forms a part of the larger science of sports psychology. Visualization is also known as mental imagery and rehearsal. Visualization is used primarily as a training tool, one that improves the quality of athletic movement, increases the power of concentration, and serves to reduce the pressures of competition on the athlete while building athletic confidence.*[11]

The theory behind visualisation is that the brain doesn't know the difference between what you're visualising, what you're imagining and what you're actually experiencing. And it allows your subconscious brain to take over. The logical part of us often stays on a fixed path and doesn't want to veer away. Whereas the subconscious, creative part of our mind, is able to explore different things and imagine different scenarios for us.

Now I'm not any sort of sportsperson, but I've found visualisation to be a fantastic tool for building confidence and answering those questions your logical brain just might not have an answer for. Lawyers are perhaps used to accessing their logical rational brain but less used to tapping into their powerful subconscious mind, where so much gold is kept.

11 Visualisation in sport, Encyclopedia.com, www.encyclopedia.com/sports/sports-fitness-recreation-and-leisure-magazines/visualization-sport.

CASE STUDY – SARAH AND JOANNE

A few years ago, I used this exercise in a workshop with Sarah an employment lawyer. In her visualisation she saw herself in meetings all day, not at her desk drafting or doing paperwork, she was instead going from one meeting to another all day long. In the visualisation she found she really enjoyed her day! Less than a year later, I wasn't surprised to hear that she'd been promoted into a more senior role that was very much client facing and team leading, and not so much of her own fee-earning work anymore.

I've also shared this exercise with a self-employed lawyer who worked predominately at home on her own. In her visualisation, she saw herself with an office outside of her home and sharing that office space with a couple of employees who she'd brought into her business. A short time later she had expanded her business and brought in at least two more lawyers.

2.4 Ready to try some visualisation?

There are some fantastic exercises for you to use in order to start defining your own version of success.

- *Perfect day visualisation* is a simple meditation process that takes you through a day in your life around 12 months from now using visualisation techniques. Sitting quietly for 5–10 minutes, consider what your perfect day would look like through to what your surroundings look like and what activities you are spending your time on.
- *Who were you as a six-year-old?* This may help to explore what's important to you and what you might want from life. Think back to your six-year-old self. What were you like as a child before the world got hold of you?

Until the age of about six or seven, we're only really aware of ourselves. It's after this age, we develop contextual 'self-awareness'. Before then it almost seems as if the world revolves around us. You'll see young children stand up to dance or sing or speak in front of people. They have no hang ups about that, no fear, because they don't fear judgement of others, there is only them and what makes them happy.

After this age we start to notice that there are other people in the world and that they could judge us, and they can ostracise us if they don't like what they see. And then through those fears, we start to change our personalities, we start to adapt in a way that makes us acceptable to other people, so that we don't feel that we are pushed out or disliked or different in some way from others. But what this can do is cause us to lose a sense of who we really are. There can be some real value in thinking about what you were like as a six- or seven-year-old child, what it was that you really enjoyed, what your personality was like, what was important to you? Sometimes by taking these cues, we can think about what it is that may be missing from our lives and what we could bring more of into our everyday.

We hope you feel encouraged to spend a little bit of time thinking about what it is that you really want out of your life. And we've given you some exercises that you can try in order to get back to the person that you truly were before the profession got hold of you.

3. What are your priorities?

It's vitally important that we spend a little time working out what is really important to us, personally, and what our personal versions of success are. As part of the conveyor belt of the profession, we can find ourselves getting up each morning and doing the same thing each day, without having any time to stop and consider what we're doing or the direction our life is taking.

It's almost as if there's no spare space in our brain, to think about anything outside of our day-to-day work, and perhaps our families as well. We're so focused on our client delivery, our client service, on meeting all of our KPIs. There almost seems to be no time left in the day for anything else. It's important if we want to see ourselves move forward in our lives, progress towards things that we want, and that will make us happy, that we actually start to work out what those things are.

It almost seems ironic that in the early part of our career, when we're thinking about A-levels, degrees, qualifications and training contracts, that we put so much of our time and energy into planning out our career and mapping out the route we're going to take and where we want to get to. But it seems to me that we reach a point in our careers where we find ourselves there. And then all of our waking hours are taken up on just running to keep up with that job and with the other demands of our lives, that we don't have time to think about what it is that we want, and the direction that we're taking. We would certainly encourage you, as a result of reading this chapter, to spend some time thinking about what it is that you want to plan out for your future.

4. How can you find and own your identity?

In this chapter we have touched on the fact that we don't like to feel different. We don't like to feel ostracised or that we stand out from the crowd. This goes back to our times as cave people, where if we were outside the group, then it was dangerous, our lives were in danger. Ironically our brains haven't changed a great deal since cave people times. As human beings we still feel that need to be accepted into the group, and that group might be our colleagues, our peers, our clients, our bosses and the management. It's in this basic human need to be accepted and to be protected as part of the group that we have historically tried to fit in and to be the same as everyone else.

You see this in the hiring and promoting decisions throughout law firms as well. It may be unconscious bias, ie, it may be that people are making decisions about who to hire or who to promote completely unconscious of the fact that they're looking for certain traits, certain personalities, certain ways of acting. Sometimes it might be conscious, it could be that people choose those that are like them. Knowing that the other people they have hired are good at that particular job, they look for people who are similar to bring into the role. It's in this way that we have historically ended up with people with the same traits, acting the same way, even thinking the same way, when actually there is real power in bringing individuality and uniqueness to the way that you carry out your practice.

Ironically, you might find that then you look back over your career and single out those particular lawyers who are very good at what they do; they may be the rainmakers, they may now be the managing partners. They tend to be people who stand out, who have something different about them, who aren't afraid to rock the boat. And, because of the fact you're reading this book, you are somebody who wants to create the best possible career and life for yourself. And as part of that, will in fact stand out from the crowd.

4.1 What is really important to you in the context of the way you live your life?

Another tool in the 'getting to know yourself better' toolkit, is values. If a vision acts as our guidance system or route map, values are the lens through which we see the world and how we make all of our decisions. Often unconsciously, we may be making those decisions if we haven't spent time working out what our personal values are. Our values drive how we assess situations, respond to others and see the world.

A sample list of values can be found within the resources on www.futureproofyourlegalcareer.com (or you can google 'sample values'). We recommend that you spend a few minutes thinking about what is really important to you. Many items on the list will seem like 'good' and useful values to you, but what is really 'you'? If we cut you in half, what values would run through you? It's important to try and distinguish between the values that society puts on us and our family and upbringing. For example, cultural norms might indicate that 'family' would be a top value. In one of my early workshops, a participant said 'family' was on her list because "well, family has to come first doesn't it". That societal or cultural norm which influenced her comment was also very evident in what we were seeing in her life. Everything came second to her commitment to her family, even her own ambitions for the future and need to do something just for herself. A few years on, I'm still amazed by how much she has changed once she understood that her values were personal to her and not what society dictated.

Values such as safety and security might be passed on from your parents or upbringing. My own father tried very hard to instil this in me, with a love for pensions and saving. However, my leading personal value of freedom won out, and so whilst I have to remain mindful of the future and our family security, my decisions are predominately made from a place of increasing a sense of freedom for myself, my children, my business and the clients I work with.

Once you have your list of values, sense check these to ensure they are personal to you and not handed down to you by expectations of society or family. Ideally you are looking for around five values – many more than this and you may find yourself struggling with competing priorities and a sense of feeling 'stuck' between a rock and a hard place.

Next consider how much time, energy and money you spend on these values. If these things are important to you, does your life reflect this? One of my property partner clients found her top value was health but when asked how much time, energy and money she spent on this value, we learnt that she worked through her lunch break, did not exercise, was eating quick convenience food and working late into the night regularly. She now goes for a walk at lunchtime, closes down by around 6pm and has completely changed her diet.

Creating a life more in line with our own values, will bring about more satisfaction, ease and ultimately success and happiness.

4.2 What about other people's values?

There is great value in understanding the individual values of those you commonly work with. If you manage a team, consider asking everyone to take part in the exercise. How you might interact with and manage a person whose top value is freedom, may differ quite significantly to someone who values recognition for example. Freddy Freedom will want as much autonomy as possible and will thrive in being given responsibility to make decisions and plan his day. Rachel Recognition will feel safe and valued by receiving regular feedback and praise. Being left alone to do her own thing may result in her feeling overlooked and like she's not performing.

5. But is visualising and goal setting a waste of time?

There is an important element to this, which is that to plan out what we really want for our future, to think about our personal version of success, and to even spend some time doing the perfect day visualisation, involves us actually stopping and stepping off that conveyor belt. And we know from speaking to many lawyers, that their sense of not doing anything (of perceived value) is a real issue for them. To feel that they're sitting doing something like meditation or visualisation or even journaling, they have a sense that they're not doing something useful, they're not doing something valuable.

This is a really common feeling amongst the profession, particularly when we're driven so hard by hourly targets. By measuring our time in six-minute units, it's very easy to see why doing 'nothing' would appear to be not a valuable use of our time. But actually, it's only in these spaces, this time of quiet and reflection, that we can actually think about our future, see what it is that we want and what it is that we want to achieve, and also receive the wisdom of how that could happen and what that could look like.

It really is a case of making some space for this once you've got to the end of this chapter. The 'future you' will thank you for it!

6. Committing to your goals in practice

Next, we are moving onto taking concrete steps towards your vision. These milestones are the route or the strategy towards your big vision – otherwise known as goals.

If you write down your goals, you are significantly more likely to achieve them.[12]

Grant Cardone, author of *The 10X Rule: The Only Difference Between Success and Failure*, attributes much of his entrepreneurial success to writing down his goals daily: "Most people are so apathetic about their goals that they only write them down once a year. As far as I'm concerned, nothing worth doing is done only once or twice a year. The things upon which your life depends most are based on the actions you take daily."[13]

Harvard Business School carried out some research into goals over a period of 10 years. Those who had written down their goals, which was about 3% of the test group, were making more money 10 years later than the other 97% all put together.[14]

There is something extremely powerful about writing down our goals. Our caveat is that we should ensure that we're not simply writing down goals that have been set, either by others or by ourselves, without any thought as to whether they are really meaningful to us, or perhaps instead if they are goals that we feel we ought to be achieving.

Once you've carried out the vision exercise and decided what it is that is in your future, whether it be 12 months or 10 years away, how do you go about putting in place the milestones in order to reach these goals? A goal without a plan is really just a wish. How can you

12 Psychology professor Dr Gail Matthews, Dominican University in California, "Goals research summary", www.goalband.co.uk/uploads/1/0/6/5/10653372/gail_matthews_research_summary.pdf.

13 Grant Cardone, *The 10X Rule: The Only Difference Between Success and Failure*, Wiley, 2011, p80.

14 Annabel Acton, "How to Set Goals (And Why You Should Write Them Down)", *Forbes*, 3 November 2017, www.forbes.com/sites/annabelacton/2017/11/03/how-to-set-goals-and-why-you-should-do-it/.

bring in some effective planning processes to really help you reach those goals?

There's a school of thinking that the most effective way to plan is in 90-day chunks. We would suggest that you have a look at the 12 months in front of you right now, and then break that down into quarters. There's probably no magic to the fact that businesses frequently plan in quarterly intervals.

Looking at what it is that you want to achieve 12 months from now, how can you break that down into what needs to be achieved at the nine-month point, at the six-month point and at the three-month point?

> *Most people overestimate what they can do in one year and underestimate what they can do in ten years.*
> Bill Gates[15]

You may have heard the story about the professor with the jar, rocks, pebbles and sand (origin unknown). A professor filled a jar with pebbles and asked his classroom if it was full, to which they replied that it was. He then proceeded to add sand to the jar and asked again if it was full, to which the response was 'yes'. Finally (in some versions of the story) he added water. But there was no room in the jar for the 'big rocks' he had on the desk.

Emptying out the jar, he instead placed in the big rocks first, followed by the pebbles, the sand and the water. Hence you may frequently find planning processes mentioning your 'big rocks'. These are the milestones which are key to the desired goal and so which need to go in first otherwise the pebbles, sand and water of life gets in the way and there is no room for the big rocks. But, if instead you plan those big rocks first, then you can add in the rest and ultimately be able to fit far more into that jar. Also, there's a huge sense of personal satisfaction that you feel when you can take off those big rocks from your list.

Never underestimate the compound effect. Don't forget that it's about small incremental steps that you take daily that will produce this

15 www.goodreads.com/quotes/302999-most-people-overestimate-what-they-can-do-in-one-year.

compound effect and bring you ultimately to the place that you really want to be.

By writing down your goals you'll be much more likely to achieve them. So, write down these goals, these big rocks, your quarterly aims and keep them somewhere that you can see them. It could be on post it notes, or something written down in your diary or notebook. It could be something on your phone or computer, but make sure you look at these regularly to remind yourself of them. If you want to become 85% more likely to achieve these goals, then find someone to be accountable to. We're frequently happier to let ourselves down than we are other people; lawyers are particularly good at this. So, by being accountable to someone we are far more likely to achieve our goals.

7. How might you manage obstacles and blocks?

One final thing we need to look at is how can you deal with obstacles and blocks that may derail you from your course. Things like this might be a global pandemic, a downturn in the economy, illness within the family, a merger or significant changes at your firm. Or it could be other blocks that people have identified to me, such as a lack of self-esteem, or self-confidence, fear of failure or not being good enough.

7.1 How can you make sure that these blocks and obstacles don't knock you too far off your path?

We need to accept that we cannot control all the circumstances around us. We can only control ourselves. We can't control everything else that happens. But we can build our resilience. We can build our positivity. And once we recognise that we may be struggling with things like self-confidence or self-doubt, then there are plenty of exercises that we can try in order to improve our results.

> *By managing fear and rejection, you gain power over them.*
> Brian Koppelman[16]

16 www.inc.com/ayse-birsel/12-powerful-tactics-that-will-help-you-banish-self-doubt-and-get-back-to-work.html.

In *Own Your Career Own Your Life*, Andy Storch says: "Your mindset has a heavy influence on your outlook on life, and that outlook influences your successes and failures."[17]

8. Conclusion

In this chapter we've looked at who you are, what's important to you, or at least how you can start to uncover some of these things if you don't know at the moment. We've looked at how you can start to plan for the future, breaking down into quarterly big rocks and how you can keep yourself accountable, and be more likely to achieve your goals. Finally, we've seen what could fall into your path and knock you off course. These things will happen for certain, but now you have the knowledge and tools to navigate your way through.

For suggestions of positive mindset exercises and tools you can bring into your everyday, please visit the resources section on www.futureproofyourlegalcareer.com.

Here are some coaching questions for you to consider:

1. What do you see yourself doing on a day-to-day basis inside your career and in your life?
2. How do you want to feel about the various aspects of your life (excited, energised)?
3. Do you want to spend more time doing a certain activity, or perhaps less time doing it?
4. What are your goals for the next 12 months?
5. What potential obstacles do you think might be in your way?
6. What steps could you take now to bring your goals to life?

17 Andy Storch, *Own Your Career Own Your Life*, Andy Storch Inc, 2020, p153.

Chapter II: Build charisma

Clare Jones

This chapter explores charisma in the context of achieving a higher-performing legal career. What is 'charisma'? Can you acquire charisma, or must you be born with it? How might you craft a strategy to develop and manage your brand and reputation?

1. What is charisma?

> *The reason we're successful, darling? My overall charisma, of course.*
> Freddie Mercury[1]

Whether you agree with this quote or not, leaders, innovators, legends and those who are generally top of their game in business often have a distinctively charismatic presence.

- Scenario 1
  Person 1 joined a discussion. They led many points but listened intently and canvassed opinion. Then this person turned to you and asked you how this issue affected your firm and whether it had impacted you personally. They talked with you, not at you, and you felt they gave you their sincere, complete and empathetic

1 www.brainyquote.com/quotes/freddie_mercury_392322.

attention. You liked this person and intended to get to know them more.

- Scenario 2

  Person 2 strutted into an event, meeting or presentation cocky, full of self-importance. Their narcissistic manner screamed: 'I'm amazing, and I know it.' They had a booming voice and made a beeline for the most important person. When they finally got to you, you experienced a bone-crushing handshake, then they asked you your name and promptly forgot it. Although you are not one to judge, you couldn't help forming an immediate negative opinion of this person.

For person 2, forced arrogance, unfortunately often rooted in chronic insecurity and a whole host of human complexities, will not win friends. Meanwhile, person 1 knew how to win friends and influence people with a quiet but arresting superpower.

1.1 How might we define charisma?

The term 'charisma' comes from the Greek language, meaning gift of grace. Some people have the effortless ability to capture hearts and minds. Whether they are famous business leaders, actors, rock stars and sportspeople, or people you've met in your daily life, they seem to have 'it'. We could argue that, whilst stylistically it presents in unique ways, Oprah Winfrey has 'it'; Bill Clinton has 'it'; Tom Hanks has 'it'; Judi Dench has 'it'; Oscar Wilde had 'it'; and Winston Churchill had 'it'.

The German sociologist Max Weber in 1947, began to use the term 'charismatic' to describe attributes of extraordinarily talented leaders who inspire devotion. He researched the degree to which leaders were attuned to their environment, the extent to which they created a compelling vision and the amount of trust they could build among their followers.

In her book, *The Charisma Myth*, author Olivia Fox Cabane presents three pillars that define charisma: presence, power and warmth.[2] Dr Ronald Riggio,[3] the leading expert and designer of the *Social Skills Inventory*, identifies the core character traits of charismatic individuals as able to express emotions, to discuss their innermost thoughts with ease, as having strong empathy and warmth as well as being discreet and able to use their intuition to understand situations. Also, they cope with emerging situations with skill, easily avoiding anger or over-reaction; they are skilled conversationalists and good public speakers; they carry themselves with grace. They get on with just about everyone, from the post-room worker to the CEO. They make us who possess less personal charisma feel rather ordinary. However, while these are laudable leadership facets, it is vital that the charisma-blessed exercise a balanced skill set. Too much emotional expression could signal overbearing instability (think Russell Brand or Robin Williams types at full tempo). Off-putting, if not exhausting.

1.2 Is charisma related to confidence?

Confidence, often aligned to charisma, is considered by a range of theorists to be one of the most influential motivators and regulators of behaviour in people's everyday lives. Very few people succeed in business without some degree of self-confidence. Confident people exude self-reliance, security and positivity. Ultimately, sure people influence others. This combination of qualities can manifest itself in a gentle, relaxed style or present a more high-energy, dynamic approach. There can be a fine line between confidence and arrogance. Some common examples include arriving late for a meeting (this comes across as rude) or optimistically thinking you can complete a project quickly, only to miss deadlines (this comes across as chaotic and insensitive).

2 Olivia Fox Cabane, *The Charisma Myth*, Penguin, 2013.
3 RE Riggio, *The Social Skills Inventory (SSI): Measuring Nonverbal and Social Skills*. In V Manusov (Ed.), *The Sourcebook of Nonverbal Measures: Going Beyond Words*, Lawrence Erlbaum Associates Publishers, 2005, pp25–33.

Appropriate, balanced confidence is where you want to be. You accept and trust your skills and abilities and have a sense of positive self-regard, yet you are not arrogant, insecure or unable to cope with criticism.

1.3 Do you need to be an extrovert to be charismatic?

What kind of people make the best leaders? Would you choose an extrovert (an animated, friendly, outgoing person) or an introvert (a quieter, more considered, reflective type)?

It's easy to stereotype charismatic people as naturally extroverted. However, ironically, introverts can be just as charismatic, or even more charismatic, than extroverts. In her book *Quiet* (2012), author Susan Cain critiques the aggressive, omnipotent style of leadership and applauds a more nuanced, gentle form of power expression.[4]

The reality is that charisma has nothing to do with introversion or extroversion. Introverts may not be quite as socially active as extroverts, but they can still be charming and eloquent. They know themselves, and they are at peace with themselves. They are also sure of themselves. This combination is magnetic. What's even more compelling is that introverts generally hate to 'big themselves up'. And the consequence is that this makes them even more attractive. Recent research highlighted by author Dan Pink in his book, *To Sell is Human*, applauds the measured and balanced presence of the 'ambivert', a person who is neither introverted nor extroverted.[5]

Indeed, contrary to popular belief, most lawyers are not extroverts. Sixty per cent are introverts, according to Eva Wisnik,[6] president of the legal training and placement firm Wisnik Career Enterprises in New York.

4 Susan Cain, *Quiet: The Power of Introverts in a World That Can't Stop Talking*, Crown Publishing, 2012.
5 Daniel Pink, *To Sell is Human*, Penguin, 2012.
6 Leslie A Gordon, "Most lawyers are introverted, and that's not necessarily a bad thing", *ABA Journal*, 1 January 2016, www.abajournal.com/magazine/article/most_lawyers_are_introverted_and_thats_not_necessarily_a_bad_thing.

Wisnik has given the Myers-Briggs personality test to more than 6,000 lawyers since 1990.

1.4 How does charisma relate to relationships?

Patsy Rodenberg, a global authority on speech in the acting world, has written several books on the subject of charisma, including *Presence*. She believes that charisma must be authentic and congruent to our true selves or it is not accurate or helpful. Her big idea presented throughout her book is that there are three kinds of 'presence' typically seen in people.[7] First circle energy is projected by people that tend to be introverted or self-absorbed. It is a rather lacklustre experience for others. Meanwhile, third circle people are powerful, overbearing and even forceful. They project their energy outwards, often to control others and situations. In between these extremes, second circle people are much more self-aware and present for others. They are naturally charming because they are authentic, genuine and have emotional intelligence. Which are you? And which do you want to be?

Bill Clinton in his book, *My Life*,[8] talked about the fact he enjoys listening to people's stories and getting to know and experience them. Perhaps being in the second circle is when we are in our natural state of curiosity, unhindered by ego or the need to climb socially. When we are present, we experience 'now' and let go of fears, thoughts and emotions. When you're fully present around other people, you're in a position of natural power and influence.

In essence, charisma is fuelled by a simple dynamic, having a relationship. Maya Angelou believed our life's work is not to improve how others feel about you; it is about making others feel better about themselves: "I've learned that people will forget what you said, people

7 Patsy Rodenberg, *Presence*, Penguin, 2007.
8 Bill Clinton, *My Life*, Knopf, 2004.

will forget what you did, but people will never forget how you made them feel."[9]

Meanwhile, Amy Cuddy, who is the presenter of one of TEDs most-watched online talks, has a different view:[10]

> *Charisma seems to be more about the intoxicating quality that you have on other people, as opposed to presence, which is more about the self-concerning others, and how you feel you represented yourself in a situation and how you were able to engage. So it's less about how others see you and more about how you see yourself.*

People with significant presence tend to be exceptional listeners. They engage with full attention, ask great questions and listen to enlist others and explore essential ideas. And there's another benefit: the ability to listen effectively demonstrates confidence.

1.5 What is the role of emotional intelligence (EI)?

Finally, perhaps we can look at the research by Dr Daniel Goleman, author of *Emotional Intelligence* (1995), who sees understanding one's own emotions as the foundation of developing one's charisma.[11] People who frequently spend time trying to understand themselves, welcome feedback from others and gain insight into their psyche, are generally more successful in business and life. Goleman's research indicates that EI is essential for those trying to build a leadership reputation.

2. Is there a 'shadow' side to charisma?

Charisma and confidence are indisputably critical attributes for success. But is having too much of these a problem? According to science, probably.

9 https://theconversation.com/how-maya-angelou-made-me-feel-27328.

10 Amy Cuddy/TEDGlobal 2012, TED Talk, www.ted.com/talks/amy_cuddy_your_body_language_may_shape_who_you_are/transcript?language=en.

11 Daniel Goleman, *Emotional Intelligence*, Bantam, 1995.

While the positive effects of charismatic communication are well researched, there are many examples of persuasive leaders that employ their communication skills for manipulative personal gain. This could be seen as the shadier aspect of leadership.[12] Sadly, politics provides us with a range of examples of this currently.

Arrogance, which could be described as an attitude of superiority, an overbearing manner or presumption, is regretfully familiar. Arrogance and charisma can be easily confused. Abuses of power and our current business environment seem to have bred some of the most arrogant leaders, both questionable in leadership style and morals. In their 2006 book, *Snakes in Suits*, Dr Paul Babiak, an expert on the scientific study of psychopathy, and Dr Robert Hare, an industrial and organisational psychologist, explore the proliferation of psychopaths in modern corporations, arguing that it is the perfect environment for the survival of reprehensible leaders or "snakes in suits".[13] In ancient Greece, 'hubris' (excessive self-regard) was considered criminal and was usually characterised by authors as backfiring with disastrous consequences. Arrogance is offensive on moral grounds and a practical level; it breeds ignorance and an 'out of touch' mentality. Equally, a surfeit of charisma can have profound consequences.

For storytellers and moviemakers, archetypes are widely used in brainstorming, crafting characters and building stories. An example of an archetype is *The Seducer*. Commonly, this character is charmingly magnetic, supremely confident, persuasive, and perhaps a little devious. Often elegant, they're provocative and mysterious, yet they can be manipulative and, at times, cynical. Common suggested professions are spy, salesman, gambler, detective, thief and, you guessed it, lawyer. The point here is not to dig at lawyers but to understand that there is probably a negative for every positive in charisma.

12 JA Conger, "The dark side of leadership", *Organizational Dynamics*, 1990, 19(2), 44–55.
13 P Babiak and RD Hare, *Snakes in Suits*, Harper Collins, 2006.

3. Are we born with charisma, or is it acquired?

You may believe that charisma is a quality that only particular people are born with, or only a lucky few have. Indeed, we are all born with unique qualities. Psychologists agree that we are vastly influenced by our environment, especially the people we are exposed to as we grow up. Enter the age-old nature or nurture debate.

It corresponds that some of the factors involved in our developing life experience will lend themselves to, and other factors will inhibit the development of, charisma. Some people who seem effortlessly charismatic were probably also exposed to multiple, early sociable experiences either at home or in education. Equally, not everyone handed the charisma 'silver spoon' will embrace social interactions and learn from these on an ongoing basis.

Charisma is perhaps a strange area to choose for a lawyer's personal development. We could have possibly chosen 'reputation', 'confidence', 'presence', 'influence' or any other magical quality. Could these, however, all lead us to the same place? We suggest that you explore how you might better your character and deal with others if possible. Acquiring deeper emotional intelligence and self-awareness is a life's work for all of us. Working on our 'charisma', whatever this means to us, regardless of our level of skill and exposure, is a choice available to everyone. Some of us will have a head start, some will learn more easily or will struggle, and others will be average learners.

4. Who has positive charisma, and why?

Although we may disagree on a definition of charisma, most people can easily spot who 'lights up the room' and who doesn't. When asked to name famous charismatic people, Martin Luther King, Nelson Mandela, Gandhi, Bill Clinton (for the umpteenth time), Barack Obama, Kanye West, Lady Gaga and Marilyn Monroe are popular choices. Is your mind racing to edit this list?

Imagine someone charismatic, whether it's a celebrity, friend or colleague. What draws you to this person? Is it because they're the most intelligent person you know, the best looking, or is it because you feel good when you are around them or hear them speak? Much of what presents itself as charisma, particularly on social media, is glossy yet shallow arrogance (whether natural or nurtured). This is neither justifiable nor useful in building a sustainable career. However, perception is a personal business. So, can you name five people you admire for their charisma, famous or not?

These individuals seem to have a 'certain something' about them. Their ability to connect with others seems intuitive yet is hard to pinpoint. People who possess charisma naturally carry a certain amount of gravitas through life, making it a breeze to step into leadership roles, motivate others and ultimately drive their success. Just how do they do it?

MIT's Human Dynamics Laboratory study (2010) explains that most charisma comes from the intangible and non-verbal aspects of our presence – such as perceived energy, positivity or tone of voice. The author Malcolm Gladwell agrees. In his best-selling book, *The Tipping Point* (2000),[14] he refers to a test that identifies those who are generally popular (even if they are shy) and influential because of their ability to transmit emotions through subtle nonverbal cues, gestures or nuances of voice. Another intangible element of charisma is the ability to connect with others; build a following; make others 'feel like he or she is the only person in the room'. Perception is indeed the reality.

5. Why should lawyers cultivate charisma?

If you research high-performance qualities, there is significant disagreement on both the volume of essential traits and their labels. The reality is that there is no 'silver bullet' when it comes to the recipe for business success, and our unique and ever-changing circumstances will have an impact. However, among the core theories that provide the basis of our current understanding of success, many agree that charisma sits in the core mix of qualities of exceptional business leaders in the competition for attention and evaluation.

14 Malcolm Gladwell, *The Tipping Point*, Little, Brown, 2000.

Building a distinctive personal brand has become a fierce competition as more professionals take advantage of the platforms available. We are all competing for audience attention. An internet connection and a distinctive viewpoint have the potential marketing capability of the world's largest brands. There is no one like you. A stand-out reputation demonstrating your personal charisma is a representation of your personality, your experiences and your values. When technology is soon able to perform much of your job, your personal brand could become your most significant professional asset.

As Jeff Bezos is widely quoted as saying: "Your brand is what people say about you when you are not in the room." In Paul Watzlawick's Theory of Human Communication (1969),[15] every relationship requires a series of intercommunications and reciprocal actions. Regardless of the intention of the messenger, a message is interpreted by the receiver and will then influence that person's response, and ultimately, this will affect the quality of the relationship. We are all in the relationship business, so thinking about your impact on others and how you relate to them is vital. The truth is that you can't communicate, so you may as well craft a considered approach to your communications that generates a positive impression. After all, your behaviour, words and actions will be noticed by others, whether consciously or unconsciously.

6. How much charisma is there in the legal profession?

The archetype of a charismatic lawyer will depend on your perspective and experience, whether your role model is trailblazing Kamala Harris or Abraham Lincoln, 'Honest Abe', paragon for equality. Perhaps you admire Ruth Bader Ginsburg or even wise-cracking Saul Goodman of *Breaking Bad* or forensic prosecutor supremo Perry Mason (substitute your role model). Beauty is in the eye of the beholder.

An article by Sally Chatterton in *The Independent* (1999), deconstructing the excellence of some of the most successful tax experts

15 Paul Watzlawick and the Theory of Human Communication, Exploring Your Mind, https://exploringyourmind.com/paul-watzlawick-and-the-theory-of-human-communication/.

in the UK, sheds some light. Technical brilliance, if relevant, is a given. Forensic excellence, being brave, creative and a tough negotiator usually goes with the territory. The elusive X-factor comes with wit, pragmatism, common sense, good humour and strong client skills. Interestingly, being a nice person may be the icing on the cake.[16]

Propagating one's charisma may horrify many lawyers, especially those who are introverted. However, perhaps this is based on a mistaken notion of what charm is? Such allure is not necessarily having the gift of gab or being 'out there'. It is more about exuding trustworthiness, being authentic and paying rapt attention to clients. That kind of charisma can spread like wildfire.

One of the most critical things in law is to achieve recognition within the legal and business community. To personify charisma, we perhaps need to look no further than a woman known simply as 'Brenda', aka Lady Hale. She was the first woman appointed to the Law Commission, the first female Law Lord, the first female Supreme Court justice and the first woman president of the Supreme Court. In her inimitable style, Brenda quietly became a household name with a killer selection of brooches.

THOUGHT LEADERSHIP

We interviewed ***Charlie Geffen****, chair of the International Stock Exchange Group, for his take on charisma. A legend in the private equity legal world, Charlie was co-chair of private equity at Gibson, Dunn & Crutcher and senior partner at Ashurst. He juggles an eclectic non-executive and trustee portfolio, including fund management, energy services, financial services, government advisory and not-for-profit.*

16 Sally Chatterton, "Market Leaders Pick Their Market Leader: Who is the text adviser with the answers?", *Independent*, 6 April 1999, www.independent.co.uk/news/business/market-leaders-pick-their-market-leader-who-is-the-tax-adviser-with-all-the-answers-1085608.html.

Charlie, charming, entertaining and insightful, is far too humble to comment on his charisma. He feels that reflecting on personal qualities is a task for others and that it will be subjective. "What is charisma to some is arrogance and pompousness to others." The path to success, he believes, requires basic competence, but the other vital character attributes include hard work, resilience and not a little luck. He cites his own experience of fortuitousness as a young lawyer: "Geoffrey Green [former Ashurst senior partner] was a real mentor to me. The personal chemistry was strong. I didn't realise until later how important it is that you fit in emotionally, but it is."

To Geffen, charisma has a lot to do with basic likability, being a good person and the term 'human obligation'. He cites research on the life regrets of older people; none repent not making more money or not having enough success; they regret a breach of personal obligation.

Considering charisma from a nature or nurture perspective, Geffen refers to neuroscience. He explains that he has learned that brain neurons are fully formed by around the age of 25 and that it is possible to change pathways and patterns, but more challenging. Therefore, at this point, personality becomes fixed chiefly. Indeed, having interviewed many lawyers, one of Geffen's critical criteria for hiring is considering how well the recruit might cope with a series of all-day meetings or a long plane journey with colleagues or clients.

Geffen believes that, for lawyers, having influence and 'presence' is most useful with clients and that being friendly and willing can go a long way. He shares wisdom from Chris Saul, former Slaughter and May veteran, and senior partner from 2008 to 2016: "[To get on in business] read *The Economist* and be curious, volunteer for things [you don't want to do]; eventually, someone will ask you to do something."

In describing the twists and turns of his (still evolving) career, Geffen perhaps shares his secret to a very natural, low-key and maybe even gentle form of charisma and the basis of building a lifelong reputation. Be cheerful and make the effort to be a person that others want to spend time with and work alongside.

7. How can charisma be measured?

Are you a natural-born charmer exuding confidence? Do people marvel at your allure and ability to interact with others? If you already think you have 'it' (charisma), that is great. Congratulations, you are a rock star lawyer! If not, don't despair. In reality, we all demonstrate charisma and confidence depending on the situation and our mood, but self-assuredness and focus on others will ebb and flow, just as we can also have moments of self-doubt and vulnerability. After all, we are only human.

At this point, it may be helpful to your current charisma to provide a starting point for understanding and honing your 'social and emotional intelligence'. So how might you do this?

7.1 Online quizzes

You only have to type some basic search terms into a search engine to discover many online quizzes you can take to analyse your charisma. Perhaps you should have a go.

7.2 Ask yourself some questions

In the meantime, here are some questions you can ask yourself to explore your charisma, inspired by academic Dr Howard Friedman and coach Janet Ioli. Perhaps scroll through the list and add your own. The perfect time to do this is after a meeting or interaction with others. You could even record an online session (with permission) to make an accurate assessment.

- How well did I enter the situation or contribute to setting the scene/agenda?
- Was I in a balanced, 'second person' mindset; personable, open and warm?
- To what extent was my appearance and non-verbal behaviour appropriate and memorable?
- Was the brief to listen/question and be curious or to talk/lecture – how did I do?
- How much did I show that I cared about their perspective and agenda?
- Did I genuinely appreciate the opportunity to interact with that person/people, regardless of their status?
- How persuasive, clear and concise was I?
- Did I share my values, vision or opinion? If so, were my ideas unique and inspiring?
- How well do I think others received my views?
- How tactfully did I handle anything unplanned?
- Did I adapt my communication intuitively to fit the person/people, time and space?
- Did I suppress negative self-talk and reaction if things got difficult?
- How relaxed, authentic and 'myself' was I?
- How comfortable was I with any silence?
- How positive and energetic was I?
- Did I make the best choices in every moment to build my charisma and presence?
- To what extent did I reflect my values?
- How might I have behaved differently on this occasion?
- What were my roles in wrapping up and decision making?
- What did I do (or agree to do) for the person/people involved?

How revealing was that exercise? Remember that no one would get off lightly if they were honest with themselves, even the most charismatic person in the world. We are all a work in progress. The purpose of self-reflection is not to promote forensic, legal-minded self-criticism but to raise self-awareness and point to areas where there may be an opportunity for self-development.

7.3 Get some feedback

The other simple thing you can do is ask others for feedback (are you cringing yet?) about your charismatic tendencies. Still, you probably know the answer to the ultimate question already: 'On a scale of 1 to 10, how charismatic are you?' Were you correct? From whom can you seek an honest opinion? How might you ask?

8. How to develop charisma

As with any other skill, some people are more charismatic than others. However, everyone can improve their charisma and presence with focus and practice. These are certainly no 'tricks', short-cuts or rules. Your appeal will evolve over some time as the impact you make on others grows.

8.1 Suggested areas of focus

As Oscar Wilde declared, "Be yourself; everyone else is already taken",[17] however, it may be helpful to have some pointers in mind when thinking about how to grow into and communicate aspects of your presence. You can break this down into five key areas as follows. Have a quick scan of Table 1 and ask yourself the questions in each section. How are you doing overall? What might you like to work on or change?

17 www.goodreads.com/quotes/19884-be-yourself-everyone-else-is-already-taken.

Table 1: How are you doing overall?

Focus	Strategy and questions you can ask yourself
1. Clarity of mind	Know yourself well. Explore your purpose, vision, values and strengths regularly to reflect on and develop your communication style: • What are your values, goals and what is important to you in business and life? • What is your superpower – the thing you do better than everyone else? • What is your favourite way to communicate?
2. Keeping the focus on others	Focus on what's in it for the other person/people: give generously, credit, reward and compliment where appropriate (but don't become a sycophant). Aim to leave others feeling heard, uplifted, informed and maybe entertained. This is also a relief to those of us who find the spotlight uncomfortable: • Who needs to get to know you? • How will you communicate with them that could be to their advantage? • What are the benefits that you can deliver to your clients?
3. Strong visual impression	You don't get a second chance to make a first impression. Whether conscious or subconscious, your visual impact is undoubtedly powerful. While you want to ensure there's nothing about your choice of clothes and grooming that distracts, you also want to be memorable and possibly distinctive: • Does your first impression reflect your values, goals and professionalism? • Is your appearance appropriate for the setting and person you are with? • What could make you stand out from the crowd?
4. Persuasive and compelling verbally	Be ready to respond creatively and intuitively to others in your everyday communications. Be ready to tell compelling stories but don't be a bore pushing your agenda. Review all of the channels (written, spoken, presenting, video, online, etc) in which you communicate and assess your skills. Ask a trusted friend for feedback on your style, and invest time in building your communication skills: • What do others say about your communication skills? • Which areas and channels are your strengths? • Which are the essential areas and channels for your audience?

continued on next page

Focus	Strategy and questions you can ask yourself
5. Align your non-verbal behaviour	Your body language is vital and can be easily forgotten. Be relaxed, open and approachable by building rapport, being attentive and reading cues. Don't forget to smile and remember you have two ears and one mouth: • What does your non-verbal behaviour say about you? • How confident and congruent are your facial expressions, eye contact, gestures, posture and tone of voice? • How could you best enhance, accent or complement your service or message with your non-verbal communication?

9. How can charisma be managed throughout a career?

Charisma and confidence are ultimately about being a leader and a great communicator who cares about others and spends a lot of time and energy engaging with them. Whilst you cannot control what other people think, this chapter will hopefully convince you that you have a great deal of control over the messages you transmit that create your personal and professional reputation. You can decide to present and conduct yourself in a thoughtful, considered way that gives others the very best of you, or you are free to act however you feel with the view that you have a right to a free form of expression.

If you intend to develop your charisma consciously and, therefore, elevate your career 'brand', then you should create a proactive plan to manage your reputation.

9.1 Have a strategy

If the development of your reputation matters to you, pay particular attention to how you may be perceived now or in future. Your brand can be enhanced or damaged by perceptions.

You can plan by considering your impact on others in any given situation, thinking carefully about what you say and share online, and preparing for how you will behave and communicate. This is not always easy when there's a deadline, but it's worth considering. You do not have to live in fear of every communication; however, you should think upfront on strategically positioning yourself.

Networking is key to building a reputation. People with solid charisma know that organisations and markets are complicated and that there will sometimes be a diversity of opinions and competing agendas. People with a strong presence are good at cultivating relationships and savvy enough to influence difficult situations positively.

9.2 Seek feedback and monitor

It's always a good idea to seek feedback on yourself as much as this may make you recoil in horror. You can do this by asking your friends and colleagues from time to time or paying close attention to any feedback provided in regular performance reviews (if you have such a thing). Equally, you can use a tool like Kevan's Johari Window (you can find this free survey online) to seek feedback on yourself actively. Also, perhaps, unfortunately, the more of a reputation you build, the more charisma is required, so you need to focus on continual improvement.

An online background check is a common practice these days, and unlike with a meeting or an interview, you can't see who is checking you out. Start by doing a Google search on yourself and see what links, profiles and images come up in the results. Don't be afraid to delve past the first two pages of results on Google. Extra links may be available on the lower pages. You can also try logging out of your social media accounts and searching for your name in each network to consider the outsider's perspective. Perhaps you will tweak your online profile to ensure a positive digital footprint.

9.3 Be ready for damage control

Having to manage your reputation might be considered a good problem to have. You've become famous, successful and achieved many of your goals. Now is the time, however, to be extremely careful about how you conduct yourself as a reputation that can take years to craft can be destroyed in minutes. Indeed, cancel culture is a new form of public ostracism and humiliation directed at individuals who are deemed to have offended others. This can take place online or in the real world, or both. If this happens to you, you will be in the business of damage control (if needed), and you might need to hire a PR consultant. Far better to avoid subtle traps in the first place.

Putting yourself 'out there' to build your success can also bring on a sense of loneliness. It's perhaps harder to build real friendships when people also may be less honest with you. Choose wise counsel and keep them close.

Success also tends to elevate the standards by which others judge you. They may envy you, resent you or even sabotage your success. You'll need to build your resilience and be less sensitive to criticism. Others may have raised expectations of you and may seek more help and support, or be demanding and hard to satisfy. That's perhaps why many lottery winners like to keep quiet. It's valuable to keep others in front of mind and bring people with you on your journey to success.

Don't dwell too much on negatives, though. Developing charisma could help you reach your career goals and positively impact lives around you and build your lasting legacy. Just make sure you guard against developing arrogant and overconfident charisma.

10. Conclusion

Now it's time to be accountable to your inner charismatic side! Here are 10 coaching questions to ask yourself right now:

1. What does the term charisma mean to me?
2. Who do I know to be charismatic?
3. What attributes do they have?
4. What is it about that person or people that I admire or notice most?
5. How would I describe my charisma (in relative terms)?
6. Is my charisma natural, or have I had to work at it?

7. What is working about my charisma now and how might I enhance that?
8. Do I think I should attempt to develop more charisma? In what way?
9. If so, what should I stop doing that is hindering my charisma?
10. How might I measure my charisma, and what might I learn?

What are the key action points you can take forward from reading this chapter and reviewing these questions?

Don't worry if thinking or talking about your charisma seems self-indulgent, superficial or just plain awkward. It's tricky for anyone vaguely decent to 'big yourself up'. No one wants to be showy or desperate, but if you don't manage your reputation, who will? It's a job to be done and number two of our essential career-building tools that will serve you well in future. Good luck. Enjoy building your devoted following. May your star shine brightly.

Chapter III: Be commercial

Hannah Beko

What does it mean to be 'commercial' in the context of being a lawyer? The Cambridge Dictionary defines 'commercial awareness' as "knowledge of how businesses make money, what customers want, and what problems there are in particular areas of business".[1] But do we see this approach when we are training lawyers to be commercially minded?

1. What is commercial awareness?

Visit YouTube and search for 'lawyers and commercial awareness'. You will find resources explaining what this means and how junior lawyers can develop commercial awareness, particularly for interview situations. There is a frequently held belief that commercial awareness means reading the newspapers, or the online equivalent, and following the business press. Does this translate for senior lawyers, or is it more than this? In truth, being commercial is a way of analysing a situation and providing the best advice and solutions for your client. It is applying common sense to the matter at hand.

1 https://dictionary.cambridge.org/dictionary/english/commercial-awareness.

One aspect of commercial awareness is knowing how to help your client make money or save money. To develop this level of attunement, you need to know your client. It is important to understand how a client's particular business works, how they make their money, or where they might be at risk of losing it. We may glean only a limited amount of this awareness from watching or reading mainstream news.

In-house legal counsel for Kentucky State University, Lisa Lang, said in an interview with me: "It's about being a business partner first, and a lawyer second. You have to understand your client's business, who their customers are, their mission and vision, and how they want to serve their customers. You layer on top of that, the fact that as a lawyer, you try to help them get to where they want to go."

You will not establish these details from newspapers alone, even if the article is about your client, their sector or their competitors. This knowledge or awareness comes from knowing the client well (please refer to Chapter V for more insights here).

Commercial awareness involves looking out for your client's best interests once you understand what these are. Perhaps finding connections amongst your network that would be useful to them and their business. In the early days of a relationship with a client, this includes fostering that relationship, asking the questions to probe into the core of their business. By asking the questions, we demonstrate commercial awareness.

2. Why is commerciality important for lawyers?

As you will see in Chapter IV on innovation and Chapter X on change, the legal profession faces a time of significant change. As this book encourages, future lawyers will need different and arguably more advanced skills in the years to come. Traditionally, lawyers were revered for their knowledge of the law. Nowadays, clients take this legal knowledge as a given, and they want to see commercial acumen demonstrated by their chosen legal team. This is what sets one lawyer/team or firm apart from another.

Clients want to know that they have the best advisers working for them to further their business objectives. As one senior lawyer explained, his first thoughts are for the board of directors and the return to the shareholders in every transaction. He might not have day-to-day contact with these individuals and only see the board at final sign-off meetings, but at that meeting he needs to be attuned to what the company expects or there will be no sign-off.

For in-house lawyers, that sense of commerciality may very well be the reason they were hired. The business looks to its legal adviser for ways to get things done. Those perhaps less commercially minded lawyers might respond with a 'no, we can't do that' in legal terms when the business wants to know 'how' they can achieve their goals. If every request from the business is met with a 'no', the in-house adviser may not be in position for long!

Lawyers have shared instances of deals being lost because of a lack of commerciality from the lawyer on the other side, with stories of clients sometimes refusing to do a particular deal if a solicitor they have come across (and had a negative experience with) is on the other side! It is undoubtedly a risk to the reputation of the individual and the firm.

THOUGHT LEADERSHIP

***Nick Gould**, a highly experienced corporate lawyer at Aria Grace, is a big believer that transactions can frequently become unnecessarily complex due to the individual lawyers involved and their personalities. This then results in the corresponding lengthy documentation and is reflected in the fees charged to the client! Here he reflects on what his clients expect from him in terms of commerciality.*

In most business areas, a product that is seen as over-complicated (probably because it's overpriced) would not succeed, and the producers or manufacturers wouldn't last long because that's how markets tend to work. However, my experience shows that our clients tend to suffer in silence in too many corporate transactions – or at least they certainly used to. I believe (actually, I have believed for years, but it is even more relevant now) that a different approach is called for when advising on and negotiating corporate transactions and certain forms of dispute resolution.

So, what should we be doing instead?

In corporate deals, I suggest the starting point should be relatively simple – advisers need to focus on the deal itself and how to get it done. On a recent multi-jurisdictional deal, the extensive set of documents were signed less than three weeks after the first draft was circulated. The clients were sophisticated, the lawyers and other advisers were commercially minded and driven by the needs of the clients. Perhaps it helped that the clients were in the same industry, and buyers and sellers wanted to get the deal done fast. No point-scoring, no late-night negotiating sessions, and a determination that we could get the deal done within a short and agreed time frame.

In the alternative, which depressingly still seems to come up all too frequently, the end result will be endless rounds of negotiations, a mess of documentation, sorted out over a long period (sometimes as long as 18 months – even on deals worth less than £250,000), and at a fee probably unacceptable to the clients, giving those clients little incentive to use the same team or firm again.

An in-house lawyer client at a FTSE 100 company once told me: "There are usually only three key issues in a legal agreement – our joint objective is to work out what they are." He also said: "It is your job to get me 90% of the way there; I will worry about the remaining 10% risk."

A commercially minded corporate lawyer should know when to say to a client: "In my experience, this is as good a deal from a legal perspective as I think you are going to get; do you want to do it?"

We shouldn't assume as lawyers that a formal 90-page document is 'better/more correct' than one less than half the length, which does the same thing and maybe does it better. I quite like the idea of letter agreements in appropriate circumstances – they are more flexible than formal and formulaic agreements.

For example, one of my clients wanted to split his engineering business with his co-owner. The co-owner's lawyer prepared a document over 30 pages long. But my client said he would only sign a document of 10 pages or less. We did it. It just needed some pragmatism, common sense and goodwill, and some smart drafting (and small typeface/narrow margins). I believe the key is to think about what the client really wants to achieve before pulling out a standard-form precedent.

This is not to say that lawyers shouldn't have views and express them. One long-standing client used to say the (only) reason he instructs me and refers me to others is that I will give him an answer. It might be right or wrong, but at least we have something to debate. As he also says, he doesn't get it right all the time – why should I!

THOUGHT LEADERSHIP

***Dr Michelle Chen**, CEO & chief strategist, Cambridge China Business Solutions, is a dual-qualified China and UK lawyer with over 25 years' experience in private organisations and government. Here she shares her thoughts on what makes a commercial lawyer.*

I love law and enjoy being a lawyer. But it's not enough to simply be a lawyer anymore. Businesses need much more. They need a trusted adviser, someone who understands the market in their sector, their challenges, their competitors, the ins and outs of how their business works and even understand the people within their organisations.

As lawyers we should be able to advise our clients with commercial sense and our legal advice should have a strategic reasoning behind it that reflects the business objectives.

My team and I offer a multi-disciplinary approach to our work. Our recent win of a high court case for a global company was on the account of our deep understanding of the client's culture and strategy. The 18-month litigation resulted in all claims being dismissed and the client ended up not having to pay a penny to the other side; it was a huge and unexpected win for our client.

Our work throughout extended further than just legal advice; our knowledge of the client's business meant we could offer support from a strategic perspective including their internal procedures and policies. Most importantly, we protected the reputation of the client's business, which we knew was their number one priority.

Senior lawyers are regularly seeing successful wins such as this one happening in pioneer law firms like ours and I believe our successes are down to the freedom to embrace the new role of a trusted adviser.

So, how can lawyers become trusted advisers? They can do so by:

- understanding the client's business and how it works;
- having a deep knowledge of the client's market sector and key jurisdictions;
- taking the time to learn and truly understand the client's business, inside and out;
- offering quality legal advice that is supported from a strategic and business perspective; and
- knowing how to apply the law to solve business problems.[2]

2 Article by Michelle Chen quoted from: https://gunnercooke.com/more-than-a-lawyer/.

For an individual lawyer's career progression, it is important that they can demonstrate awareness in relation to their clients and the environment in which they operate. As a valued member of your firm, it is also expected that you will have an understanding of the pressures your firm is facing and its plans for the future. How might changes in the economy and the world impact your firm and its client base? Can you make sure your finger is on the pulse concerning potential changes and stay ahead of the curve to keep your firm competitive?

3. What value does commercial awareness have?

3.1 Referrals and repeat business

Being commercial in such a way as to listen to the client's needs and their preferred method of doing business can very often make all the difference between retaining that client, creating a long-standing relationship and even having them recommend you to others. Much of a senior lawyer's business may be via recommendations and referrals, so how do you put a value on that?

Whilst the family and probate lawyers amongst us may not rely very heavily on repeat business, they will certainly rely on recommendation and word of mouth and develop relationships with referral partners such as accountants and financial advisers.

> *Firms can boost their profits by up to 100% by retaining just 5% more of their clients. Increasing customer retention rates by 5% increases profits by 25% to 95%.*[3]

It is much easier to generate work from an existing client than to bring in a new one. To refer to the Pareto Principle,[4] 80% of your profit comes from 20% of your clients. Demonstrating to a client that you

3 Frederick F Reichheld and W Earl Sasser, "Zero Deflections: Quality Comes to Services", *The Magazine*, Harvard Business Review, September–October 1990.

4 Vilfredo Pareto, *Cours d'Économie Politique: Nouvelle édition par G-H Bousquet et G Busino*, Librairie Droz, Geneva, 1964.

understand their business and their sector is what you might call high-level commercial awareness. Your client needs to know that you know them, as a person, what they want from the deal and how they want it to happen, getting into the detail of their commercial reality.

3.2 Cost savings for the client

US in-house counsel Lisa Lang shared in a discussion with me how her legal team is expected to find ways to save the University money. Lisa refers to the example of supplier payment contract terms. The University would commonly allow payment terms of 30 days, but many of their outgoing supply contracts required payment within 10 days. This was costing the University money in terms of late payment fees. Liaising with the purchasing and invoicing departments and carrying out a contract and terms review meant that when new contracts are negotiated, the legal team could improve the University's position and save money.

Perhaps not always considered to be the role of a lawyer, how much more valuable is a lawyer who can advise not only on the legalities of their client's position but how much the client could save by taking a particular action or avoiding one? It is thinking outside the box.

4. How can you develop your commercial awareness?

How do we develop and improve any skill? With practice. Commercial awareness at the high level mentioned earlier in this chapter can be cultivated by following the news and updates about your client's industry, sector and even within the client company if the information is readily available in the public domain.

As lawyers of the future, what is required is a much deeper level of awareness than simply what is available in the public arena. We need a good awareness of the client's personality (both their business and the person immediately giving the instructions). How they do or do not like to work. For example, are they detail people or do they prefer brief bullet points? What is their personal and company attitude towards risk?

4.1 Asking the silly questions

You can demonstrate in the early stages of a new relationship that you are willing to put in the work to get to know them by asking appropriate questions and listening carefully. It is often the simple or the 'silly' questions that elicit the level of detail you might be looking for. Lawyers may be wary of asking questions that they believe they 'should' already know the answer to, or which might be considered to be too obvious. There can be a fear that it would somehow expose them as not being the expert, not having all of the information. But, it's often in examining these questions that perhaps no one else is asking that we can identify the real motivations and drivers for clients enabling us to advise them better.

4.2 Adopting a coaching approach

It can be helpful to adopt a coaching mentality with your clients by asking inquiring questions about their business, the transaction or deal they are discussing, and how this fits into their business's general plans. If something isn't relevant, the client will no doubt say so, but more often than not they will appreciate the fact that you've asked and been interested in how the piece of work you are engaged in impacts upon the bigger picture. Very rarely does one transaction affect a business in isolation.

4.3 Getting to know the person/people behind the business

Taking time to foster a personal relationship with your instructing client (at the level you and the client are comfortable with, of course) enables you to develop a unique insight into the personal concerns and priorities of the client so that you can advise and deliver work in the way that suits them best. Understanding how they like to communicate, their style and preferred method, and adapting your own to fit with them is a demonstration of your knowledge of them as a person, their preferred way of working and their business needs.

CASE STUDY

In the early part of my career, I worked predominantly with one corporate client and had monthly meetings with two instructing clients. Over time I came to know them very well on both a personal and a business level. I understood the way they liked to work and how they wanted me to communicate with them. They were very professional but time poor. They appreciated short and succinct communications from me where I had done most of the work for them, which they simply needed to approve or amend as necessary.

I worked alongside a lawyer who took an entirely different approach and chose to correspond with them in very long communications asking lots of questions about what they wanted to do. I believe the strong relationship I developed with them was based not only on our personal connection but also my realising what they needed from me as a legal adviser and providing this service to them, thereby making their own day-to-day work lives easier.

Another lawyer could have done exactly the same work for them and achieved the same results perhaps, but I like to think that our relationship was also strengthened by the value I added in terms of saving them precious time.

4.4 Understanding business generally

It is now easier than ever to understand the drivers of business leaders, CEOs of top companies. By listening to podcasts, interviews, TedTalks and so on from business leaders, we can gain further insight into how the people at the top make their decisions, assess risk and sometimes even what they do and don't want from their legal teams!

As you progress in your career, you are likely to need to demonstrate to your firm that you understand the business of legal services and that of your client. Individuals are expected to show their understanding of the business they are involved with and how that business fits into the bigger picture of legal firms locally and nationally when they are looking to progress. Historically there may have been such a high level of competition between firms, between lawyers even, that getting an insight into other businesses was not easy. Now that businesses are far more open, articles are released regularly on social media; it is much easier to follow what might be regarded as your competitor businesses, to see what you can learn from them to improve your legal practice.

5. How can you demonstrate your commercial awareness to others?

When we run our practices/transactions with commercial awareness, this will be demonstrated in our communications with the other side and our client and the drafting, negotiation and finalising of documents. This deep level of awareness would (it is hoped) lead to less protracted negotiations. If you know the baseline your client is willing to accept regarding the fundamentals of a deal and what your client's non-negotiables are, it is hoped the deal can run to its conclusion more smoothly.

Working with counterparts is a great compliment when your opposite number on a transaction recommends you down the line. Why do they do this? Because they admired how you handled the transaction, perhaps you made their life easier, and the matter run more effectively because of your approach.

Nick Gould told me that it's important to "compromise, work to find positive solutions and do the deal if you think you can. In short, utilise that under-rated skill of common sense". This is perhaps where the lawyers who value commerciality over detail (for the sake of details) will stand out from those who follow the letter of the law and become bogged down in detail.

Here are some practices you might adopt to both improve your commercial skills and also demonstrate to the client that the detail of their own business is vitally important to you:

- Do you debrief a transaction with the client and your team afterwards and learn where it might have run more smoothly?
- Ask your client for feedback on how the whole process might be improved next time from their perspective.
- If they are a new client to you, do you ask them at the outset how they like to work, what they expect in terms of updates, presentation of information, reports and timescales? Can you get a sense from them as to whether they are a detail person or a high-level review person?

6. How can you respond to your client from a commercial rather than a legal perspective? Why should you?

This may be one of the significant shifts often found the hardest for lawyers as they move from a more junior to a senior position in their career. For years we learn about the law, the legislation, the cases, the correct way to draft documents and to run matters. But a commercially minded client takes all of this as a given. They don't want chapter and verse unless they are a detail person, of course, and you need to know if your client is one of those.

What the client wants is an answer. They want to know: can I do what I want to do? If not, how do I do the next best alternative? In short, they do not want a 'no' person, unless, of course, there really is no other answer!

This involves stepping into the client's shoes, seeing everything from their perspective, through the lens of their business and what they are trying to achieve, taking all of the facts into account. To do this effectively, you need to make the client's business your business.

Consider an approach by which you weigh up your knowledge of the law (in the background) and ask yourself what options your client has in their situation they find themselves in? What would be their best option? Not necessarily from a legal point of view, but from a commercial one?

Debate it, discuss it with your client. If there are a number of options, both legal and commercial perhaps, be a business partner to the client. Sit down and discuss the various options, the pros and cons and likely outcomes of each. Work with the client as their board of directors would do to reach the best decision for them.

Don't be afraid to give an opinion. It might seem counterintuitive to a lawyer, who is perhaps used to setting out the legal position and the legal options. But, taking all of that into account, set out what you would recommend as your client's best course of action. It's perfectly acceptable to be clear that this is your advice from a personal perspective rather than a legal one. For example, a client might have a strong case legally and on principle ought to pursue their rights and seek compensation. At what point can (or should) their lawyer advise whether fighting a particular battle is not in the best interests of the client, from a personal or wellbeing perspective?

For junior lawyers moving into a more senior position, there can be an uncomfortable period where you move from wanting to please the client by doing what they ask. Being commercial might include pointing out that the proposed solution might not be the best option for them. This might involve disagreeing with them, politely and respectfully of course, but not being afraid to express your ideas in the client's best interests.

7. How can you get to know your client?

Be genuinely interested in them, ask the questions, take time to get to know them. This might not be compatible with immediate profitability. Compare the options of simply finding out which documents a client needs, taking instructions, drafting and sending them for signing. As compared against, hearing from the client what they believe they need and inquiring into why they need this, the circumstances surrounding the deal and the client's business plans more widely. It will incur more time to take the second option, which is arguably why some lawyers don't do this as part of their practice. But this approach means that you might identify a different way of handling the same situation, which is preferable for the client.

Become a business partner for your client. Rather than discussing only the aspects of the deal or project you are working on, take every opportunity to learn more about other areas of the business, which might, of course, aid internal referrals inside your firm, but more importantly, allow you to get closer to the client and understand the ins and outs of their business better than other legal advisers might. Again, this approach may not be immediately compatible with profit. It might not be chargeable, but what value do you place on having strong relationships with your clients that go beyond the superficial day-to-day working knowledge that others may have?

8. What matters to your client, and why?

Many businesses in the current climate value cost transparency and certainty. A property developer shared that regardless of the fees agreed at the outset, his board instructed him to negotiate on these fees at the end of the matter. Clients are much more cost-conscious than they have ever been. The client themselves is likely to be under pressure from their employer/board/shareholders concerning fees. Understanding the parameters in which they can instruct you will allow any difficult costs conversations to be had more smoothly.

As many alternative business structure firms (including gunner*cooke*) have found, their clients value the knowledge that a senior lawyer is handling their matter. They will not be paying for training or supervision time (that's a cost to the firm if they want to develop their internal talent). They will always be able to speak to the lawyer who has day-to-day conduct of their matter and is fully up to speed, hopefully meaning that the matter can proceed more swiftly.

9. What are the most significant issues facing clients now and in the future?

Getting to know your client and their business at the deeper level we have discussed enables you to have an eye to the future. Depending on the sector in which you work, what changes to legislation, society or culture do you envisage? How do you see these anticipated changes might impact on your client? Where can you add value to the client by considering such changes ahead of time and seeking to protect your client's position wherever possible? Of course, it is not the role of a lawyer to predict the future; as trusted business advisers, where do we see opportunities to aid our clients in staying ahead in their businesses?

10. Conclusion

Being commercial, therefore, is not only concerned with your knowledge of the law or the tactics of the matter in front of you. Rather, consider developing a deeper understanding of your client coupled with a willingness to adapt your style and way of working to one which benefits the client in terms of what they are trying to achieve overall. In reviewing this yourself, here are some questions for you to consider:

1. What do you consider commercial awareness means to you as a lawyer, to your clients and your firm?
2. How has the meaning of commercial awareness developed as you moved from an aspiring lawyer to an experienced legal adviser to your clients?
3. How would you educate a new trainee or paralegal on the meaning of commercial awareness if they were working with you?
4. How would you encourage them to develop their sense of commercial awareness?

When considering your practice in terms of your commerciality:

1. Who are your: a) most profitable clients and b) most long-standing clients?

2. How has your commercial awareness of these clients' businesses and personalities aided you in retaining them and developing that relationship?
3. What more could you learn about them?
4. What further questions could you ask to demonstrate your interest in your clients' way of doing business?

Chapter IV: Be innovative

Hannah Beko

In this chapter we will examine innovation in the legal profession. What does this mean for lawyers and law firms? As a profession which tends towards tradition, do we need to consider innovation at all? What types of changes should be considered, and how can a lawyer further their career by identifying more innovative opportunities in their practice?

> *There is one inescapable reality both in life and in business, which is that change is constant, there's always going to be change. If you don't embrace it, you're going to have a difficult time. If change is constant, perhaps we ought to be innovating and getting ahead of that change before it's forced upon us.*[1]

1. How do we define innovation in the context of the legal profession?

The Oxford English Dictionary defines 'to innovate' as "to make changes in something established, especially by introducing new methods, ideas, or products". Originating in the 1590s, the etymology of the word means to "bring in new things, alter established practices".[2]

1 Tariq Mubarak, interview with the author.
2 www.etymonline.com/search?q=innovate.

The altering of established practices is an interesting turn of phrase when we consider innovation in the context of the legal profession. There may be advancements which are no longer considered innovative in the world in general, but which could be regarded as 'new' in law. Perhaps it is a disservice to discount those advances that might be well entrenched elsewhere, but which are genuinely different to 'business as usual' when it comes to practising law.

It is a common assumption that when we talk about innovation, we are talking only about legal technology. Then comes a frequently held opinion that this means big changes involving the replacement of legal professionals with artificial intelligence. AI may have been a concern of lawyers for some time but we are yet to see this materialise as a reality. The concerns may however have had a negative impact on the adoption of some technology. Law firms may try to bring in new systems, but without the adoption of these systems by the lawyers, they are unlikely to prove effective.

For increasing numbers of lawyers to adopt innovation into their practices, Lisa Lang (in-house counsel at Kentucky University) believes we need to alter our definition.

> *Innovation means to do things differently than what you've done before. A lot of the time that involves technology. But sometimes we limit ourselves by defining it in terms of technological advancements. Part of the problem for in-house legal counsel (for example) is that we don't always have the funds and the resources available to us. We don't necessarily have the money to buy all of the best and brightest technology. This leads people to say we can't be innovative, because I have no budget. I would say that this is defining innovation too narrowly. There are things you can do to be creative in your processes that doesn't require money and technology but improves efficiency and effectiveness.*[3]

3 Lisa Lang, interview with the author.

And according to commercial property lawyer, Tariq Mubarak, innovation may simply mean "looking at service delivery in a more evolved kind of way".

In addition, of course, innovation will look very different in different places. The legal profession ranges from sole practitioners through to large multinational companies and their adoption and rate of innovation may be surprisingly different as we will examine later.

2. Why is innovation in the legal industry important?

There are many reasons why innovation needs to be embraced, perhaps more than ever before. In this section, we will explore how innovation is required to cope with change, keep pace with other sectors, stay viable and competitive, and potentially aid a profession struggling with burnout and stress on levels higher than the general population.

2.1 To remain competitive and viable

US in-house counsel Lisa Lang told me that her department needs to be innovative because they are viewed as a cost centre: "You either save the company money, or you make money. We have to start utilising technology to do it better and to be more efficient."

Innovation, therefore, may not be big, shiny or expensive but involves small tweaks that cumulatively make a difference to the business. Innovation may mean identifying and actioning seemingly small tweaks or improvements which demonstrate further added value in the case of in-house legal counsel for example.

> *If you don't innovate, and you just practise the law, when a company is going through a lean period, often the general counsel or legal department is one of the departments they look to let go or outsource. You don't innovate just because others are doing it; you do it because you need to do it in order to stay competitive and viable.*[4]

4 Lisa Lang, interview with the author.

In-house lawyer Laura Jeffords Greenberg for Unity Technologies[5] says the biggest reason we need to innovate is to keep up with business. As in-house counsel, she sees the need for her to communicate effectively with the business she supports. The legal team need to understand the business and the tools they are using, and similarly the business needs to understand how the in-house team can support them.

In times where businesses are increasingly cost conscious, innovation can be a way to deliver costs savings and demonstrate that lawyers are actively looking for ways to improve their client's bottom line.

2.2 Stress and burnout

Perhaps not immediately associated with innovation, the writers believe that we should ask whether a profession with documented high levels of stress and mental ill health, ought to look outside of the profession for opportunities to improve the situation for lawyers.

At Unity Technologies, Laura explained that they are working on asynchronous communication. For the not so IT literate amongst us, this means non-real-time communication. So when we are speaking directly to someone in real-time, this is synchronous communication, ie, we're communicating at the same time. Messaging, emailing or communicating via LinkedIn, for example is asynchronous communication, and you do not expect a response from someone immediately.

A limit on real-time communication in the current world is important for both wellbeing and efficiency. When we are switching our attention from one thing to another constantly throughout the day (such as drafting a document and then noticing an email pop up on the screen) we are not using our time efficiently and are actually losing the time it takes to refocus onto the task in hand once you've sent that quick email response. It also heightens the stress response, which over time can be damaging.

I think connectivity can go too far. That's why we all get stressed and tired out. We're also dealing with a US company and so have issues with

5 A leading platform for creating and operating interactive, real-time 3D (RT3D) content.

time zones, we are looking at solutions, and one of these is asynchronous technology which is just a new way of saying you don't expect an immediate response. This also allows the person to have that deep thinking time, so they don't get burned out and have the headspace to really critically think through all of the issues.[6]

There are some interesting points to consider here around solving the time zone issue, allowing professionals to have the time to work intensely on a matter, which produces a superior result, and has an upside in terms of improving stress levels as well.

Whilst in some ways non-real-time communication, such as emails and messages, are not new, a willingness to accept that these are asynchronous and we do not expect an immediate response, would potentially be a welcome development. This is a form of mindset innovation which we will consider further in this chapter.

Some questions to consider:

- Why do you think the profession needs to look for opportunities to innovate?
- What has been the legacy to date of our failure to innovate as other industries have done?
- Why is it important for both firms and individual lawyers to look for ways to innovate?

3. What are the different types of innovation?

3.1 Technology

Undoubtedly a large part of recent and, no doubt, future innovations in the profession, will involve legal technology. This might be time recording software, dictation programmes or improved CRM systems. Whilst anything which saves a lawyer time is a positive, we might need to avoid seeing legal technology as the panacea to an array of the profession's problems, like time management issues and burnout. Whilst

6 Laura Jeffords Greenberg, interview with the author.

these tools might ultimately prove useful, firms need to ensure they will have widespread acceptance and adoption of new technologies and that they do in actuality improve the day-to-day lives of fee earners.

There is a place for useful technology that saves the lawyer time and perhaps improves wellbeing, and goes towards reducing risk in transactions by taking more of the burden away from the lawyer.

3.2 Culture

There are a few particular elements of the common cultures seen in law firms which, in the view of many, require innovation or indeed, a change away from what was previously considered established practice. The first of these is the so-called 'blame culture'.

There are many professions that take a different approach to mistakes. They will seek to learn and perhaps even innovate rather than to look out for someone to blame. The legal profession in the main can be very different. There can be an unwillingness and perhaps even a paralysing fear around making mistakes. This can lead to hiding of errors, attempts to brush them under the carpet and, perhaps worse, an attempt to deflect blame elsewhere, often onto a junior colleague or supervisee.

> *It highlights the need for a growth mindset in life. It advocates for changing attitudes towards failure, and understanding that the only way we learn is by trying things and altering our behaviour based on the results.*
> Richard Branson, Virgin Group[7]

Blame is not the only aspect of legal practice culture that requires modernisation. In *To Innovate or Not to Innovate*[8] Darryl Cooke talks about the practice in City firms referred to as 'beasting' junior lawyers. The idea that they will be worked into the ground, will sink or swim, whilst the equity partners maintain a very healthy income from that model. This is just one aspect of the prevalence of poor mental health

7 Matthew Syed Consulting, "Black Box Thinking: The Surprising Truth About Success", www.matthewsyed.co.uk/resource/black-box-thinking-the-surprising-truth-about-success/.

8 Darryl Cooke, *To Innovate Or Not to Innovate*, Globe Law and Business, 2019.

amongst lawyers. Attitudes towards mistakes and errors, the need for better physical and mental health support and an understanding of the common mindsets found in law would be a very welcome area for further innovation for the benefit of the individuals and the businesses in which they work.

3.3 Inclusion

Separate to the issue of culture is the very real problem of a lack of inclusion within law.

In 2019 the Law Society reported on the under-representation of women and black, Asian and minority ethnic lawyers at senior levels:

- *The proportion of women solicitors working in private practice increased to 49% in 2019, but the proportion of private practice partners that are women was 31%.*
- *Just 18% of women in private practice are partners compared to 40% of men.*
- *35% of white private practice solicitors were partners compared to 25% of BAME solicitors.*[9]

The issue of a lack of inclusion at senior levels is an important one. Senior levels are the decision makers, the shapers of the future; without inclusion at these levels, further change will be even further away. There is also plenty of evidence to the fact that more diverse and inclusive organisations are better places to work and produce higher profits; they are generally more innovative!

3.4 The chargeable hour

The process of charging by the hour has long come under scrutiny. Arguably it does not serve the clients and does not help the lawyers who

9 Diversity Profile of the Solicitors' Professions 2019, The Law Society, 25 November 2020, www.lawsociety.org.uk/en/topics/research/diversity-profile-of-the-solicitors-profession-2019.

work longer and longer hours to reach their required targets with little consideration as to the quality of their output throughout the working day or week. More and more clients are recognising that this way of billing is not in their favour and are asking for (or demanding) fixed fees.

As an in-house lawyer, Laura shared that when she's managing a project, she needs to know what the legal cost is going to be. It doesn't matter how many billable hours it takes; she agrees with her providers the scope of the project that needs delivering within the agreed cost. This way, the interests of the client and service provider are far more aligned.

It may be quite some time before the larger firms agree to work without the chargeable hour but many new model firms and alternative business structures are adopting this approach so it may be a matter of time before this becomes obsolete.

3.5 Working from home

At the time this book was envisaged, it was pre-global pandemic, and although the themes and ideas in the book very much stand alone, in this area perhaps it would be impossible not to mention the effect of 2020/2021 on the legal profession.

In Tariq Mubarak's words, "the pandemic has lit a firecracker in terms of moving us forward much more rapidly in terms of working from home".

For many years lawyers have been asking for more flexibility, agile working and autonomy over where they work. This is not exclusively from women with families. Those with children and without have been seeking more freedom from the daily commute and presenteeism constraints for some time. This change may have happened far more slowly if it were not for the pandemic.

A lack of trust was perceived to be the biggest issue, which the pandemic has gone quite some way to counteract. There had been a historic feeling amongst traditional firms that staff needed to be visible in the office. A crazy notion really for a group of highly talented, highly educated and highly driven individuals as tend to be attracted to law!

This change in the practice of law which cannot now be un-done post-pandemic, is yet to be fully realised but is an extremely welcome innovation for many.

3.6 Employment relationship

The pandemic changes have not only altered the future of working from home for lawyers but also increased the pace at which legal professionals might seek to redesign their careers and map out their lives.

Laura highlighted the need for the profession to think about innovating in terms of the way individuals are treated. There is a growing sense that the attitude prevalent after the global financial crash in 2008/2009, ie, you are lucky to have a job at all, may not be accepted as it perhaps once was. It will become increasingly important for firms to decide how they want to be perceived in the market place in terms of a place to work.

The hiring process may also be shifting towards a more values-based approach. Increasingly, firms and teams are looking for candidates who display initiative, problem-solving, good interpersonal skills and whose personal values fit with those of the firm/organisation or team. (You might want to refer back to Chapter I in terms of articulating your own values.)

3.7 Mindset

Along with the many established traditions of our profession, certain mindsets or ways of thinking, have become entrenched. This is probably due to the hiring, training, role modelling and promoting practices of the past. With or without meaning to, many firms have been hiring and promoting for the same traits and tendencies, the same patterns of thinking.

> *You have to now innovate your mindset. You have to be willing to accept that we're moving away from the traditional way of working.*[10]

10 Tariq Mubarak, interview with the author.

This book will go a long way towards helping you to evaluate your current mindset and identify the opportunities for development for both yourself and your team. Here we suggest some questions to help you start this thought process:

- How has the pandemic changed your attitude towards your work–life integration?
- Looking around your team or firm, how diverse and inclusive is it at each of the various levels of management? Do you consider this needs improvement and is there a part you can play in this change?
- What are your values? Look back at Chapter I and perhaps explore those of your immediate team and how these fit with the wider values of the organisation.

4. Is disruption the same thing as innovation?

According to Professor Clayton Christensen, the leading expert in disruptive innovation, disruption is not the same as innovation:

> *Disruptive Innovation is not a breakthrough innovation that makes good products a lot better. But it has a very specific definition, that is, it transforms a product that historically was so expensive and complicated that only a few people with money and skill had access to it. A disruptive innovation makes it so much more affordable and accessible that a much larger population can have access to it.*[11]

Professor Christensen typically uses this example to explain the idea of disruptive innovation. He refers to the world of computer technology. Initially, there was one mainframe computer at Manchester University, worth around £2,000,000. Next came home desktop computers worth around £2,000, and finally, we now have the smartphones worth under £200. Now the vast majority of people have access to this technology as it has been produced on a larger scale, more cheaply and is useable by everyone even if they are not a computer whiz.

11 Disruptive Innovation Explained by Professor Clayton M Christensen, www.youtube.com/watch?v=qDrMAzCHFUU.

4.1 How could this apply to the legal profession?

We are not advocating the reduction of the costs of legal services just because they are being provided by an alternative business structure – a lawyer's experience is their experience. As one ABS firm founder said to one of his new partners who'd recently left a large City firm and was now charging a lower hourly rate as a result, when you walked over that bridge between your old office and the new one, did you get worse at your job? No – then there is no justification for charging less.

But I think innovation has a part to play here. In my opinion, we should not be offering the same services at a lower cost, although we should be looking for ways to allow small business start-ups to access good legal advice and services at a price that makes it possible for them to do so. A new business on a shoestring budget cannot invest thousands in advice on their website policies or their terms and conditions of sale, yet should they be left entirely without advice? No.

What this requires is innovation in the way services are provided, into a one package model, which can be delivered to many at a lower cost. This is exactly what former lawyer to Richard Branson, Suzanne Dibble created in her Small Business Legal Academy. A relatively low-priced package of legal documents created for small businesses to get the protection they could not otherwise afford and would therefore have gone without.

Suzanne shares:

[Start ups] are investing time and effort in [their] business, and it deserves to have the legal protection that it needs and the legal structures that can help it to grow. The consequences of ignoring it or getting it wrong can be far reaching, long lasting and very expensive. I have developed my business around helping small business to legally protect themselves in the most simple and affordable way possible.[12]

This is disruptive in the sense of the definition coined by Professor Christensen. An entirely new product, not legal services delivered the

12 Suzanne Dibble, https://suzannedibble.com/.

way it's always been delivered, to those who can afford it. There are others following in these footsteps. I have often considered opening 'leases online' but never had the time to do it! As more and more lawyers are thinking more 'innovatively', we are seeing YouTube guidance videos and short courses being created to give generic advice as a starting point for those businesses just trying to get off the ground.

Ask yourself some coaching questions:

- Do you consider the way legal services are traditionally provided requires updating?
- Is the profession 'fit for purpose' in the modern age in your opinion? If not, why not and what adaptions would you like to see?
- Do firms need to consider the future when planning their offerings?
- Should you as an individual lawyer look for ways to innovate your individual practice and/or the way your team works?

5. How can lawyers identify opportunities to innovate?

Innovation can come from the most straightforward improvements. As we've already identified, some innovations (such as the Scottish Land Register portal in 2009) might be brand new, expensive and different, but if they don't make anyone's life easier, no one will adopt them and they will disappear.

Innovations might include small improvements that simply make a lawyer's life easier. We are seeing, for example, technology that deals with missed telephone calls and converts these into a text conversation. Lawyers are increasingly adopting diary-scheduling software for making client appointments and considering ways to better manage their email inbox. Any time-saving device is likely to be valuable: if lawyers can start saving minutes in an hour, hours in a week and weeks in a year, this is big!

Some questions to help you to identify possible areas for you to innovate in your work:

1. Where do you spend time doing something in your everyday work that could be done better, more effectively or efficiently, saving you time or reducing risk?
2. What is a bugbear in your everyday work routine, that could be improved?
3. Where have you experienced systems or processes elsewhere that you think might benefit you or your team?

6. How can lawyers become innovative?

Do refer back to Chapter I, where we considered values and interests, what makes you, you. One commercial property lawyer (as I am) is very like another commercial property lawyer, save for our personality and who we are. Being a lawyer can often start to define us and our identity. We look to role models and those who have gone before us and imitate them to a degree as we find our way. Innovation will not happen like this, and we need to dig into who we are as people. What can we learn from our outside hobbies and interests that might benefit our everyday work?

Tariq Mubarak suggested it is about going back to your old passions to be more creative in your thinking. It's also about looking outside the profession for ideas and inspiration. When we are surrounded by the same people every day and doing the same things, it can be hard to be creative or innovative.

Ask yourself where can you look for opportunities to meet new people and experience new things? It could be that in pursuing an outside interest, you encounter a new network of people or different business types for example.

We can also look to the new entrants and the more junior members of our profession. These individuals have grown up with different technology and have different expectations of the world of work and its place in their life.

Thought River, the Contract Acceleration Platform, uses AI to help lawyers identify contract issues more swiftly. In the pandemic they have adopted 'reverse mentoring' whereby the junior staff would train their supervisors on the newest technology for keeping in touch remotely. This not only strengthened the relationship between the two and gave the juniors more confidence, but the senior staff also learned new skills.

Lisa Lang believes that lawyers should "dig in and learn". When she needs to learn about something new, she will go to webinars, read articles, review what others are doing; it's about learning what's out there and how you can make it applicable to your everyday.

- What outside interests do you have, or have always wanted to pursue? Inspiration can come from the most unexpected places!
- What downtime do you have? Our most creative and innovative ideas rarely come to us while we're sitting at our desks. If you want to access your creative side, you will need to spend some time away from the computer and the telephone.

7. How is diversity relevant to innovation?

The law has an issue with diversity and inclusion, which it is working hard to address. Not only is this important because it is the right thing to do, but from a growth perspective, diversity has been shown to increase the rate of innovation.

> *Inherent diversity [traits you are born with], [however] is only half of the equation. Leaders also need acquired diversity [traits you learn through life experience] to establish a culture in which all employees feel free to contribute ideas. Six behaviors, we have found, unlock innovation across the board: ensuring that everyone is heard; making it safe to propose novel ideas; giving team members decision-making authority; sharing credit for success; giving actionable feedback, and implementing feedback from the team. Leaders who give diverse voices equal airtime are nearly twice as likely as others to unleash value-driving insights, and employees in a "speak up"*

culture are 3.5 times as likely to contribute their full innovative potential.[13]

No matter who or where they are, if people feel a sense of belonging and are valued by their employers for their unique contributions, perspectives and circumstances, they are empowered to innovate more.[14]

8. What is the 'innovation mindset'?

Earlier in this chapter we looked at the need for lawyers to innovate their mindset, the culture and previous ways of thinking. What is an innovation mindset?

Accenture,[15] a global strategy consultancy, sets out the "Six Elements of an Innovation Mindset" as being:

1. Purpose: getting staff aligned to and supportive of the firm's purpose.
2. Autonomy: encouraging a culture of change, and trust to see change through.
3. Resources: having the necessary tools, time and incentives to innovate.
4. Inspiration: finding inspiration from outside the firm (or the profession).
5. Collaboration: working across the firm with other departments/ colleagues in harmony.
6. Experimentation: trying out new ideas without being afraid of failure.[16]

13 Sylvia Ann Hewlett, Melinda Marshall and Laura Sherbin, "How Diversity Can Drive Innovation", *The Magazine*, Harvard Business Review, December 2013.

14 Ellyn Shook and Julie Sweet, Accenture, "Getting to Equal 2019: Creating a Culture That Drives Innovation", www.accenture.com/gb-en/about/inclusion-diversity/gender-equality-innovation-research.

15 Accenture is a leading global professional services company, providing a broad range of services and solutions in strategy, consulting, digital, technology and operations: www.accenture.com.

16 Ellyn Shook and Julie Sweet, Accenture, "Getting to Equal 2019: Creating a Culture That Drives Innovation", www.accenture.com/gb-en/about/inclusion-diversity/gender-equality-innovation-research (paraphrased).

Some of these elements do not come perhaps naturally to those in the legal profession. But, by adopting some of the suggestions in this chapter, we may come a little closer towards this innovation mindset.

9. Why does innovation fail and what we can learn?

There are potentially a number of barriers in relation to innovating in law firms, especially the more traditional organisation, in which change is frequently likened to turning an oil tanker. Of course, this doesn't mean that we should write it off as an impossibility. Still, there will be different rates of innovation in the different structures of legal service providers, as suggested at the start of this chapter.

It might be a cliché to suggest that lawyers are afraid of change, but we tend to be risk-averse. There is an element of resistance to change rather than a willingness to embrace it. There might also be a certain level of 'innovation fatigue' as firms have been introducing changes and innovations which perhaps are either not particularly effective (just because something is tech doesn't mean it's an improvement) or are not properly implemented as buy-in is not encouraged across the whole firm.

Many lawyers have seen the adoption of systems intended to be revolutionary, but which failed to meet expectation. For example, in 2009 the Registers of Scotland trialled a new online portal, enabling them to carry out Automated Registration of Title to Land (ARTL) transactions. The intention was that an ARTL transaction would save money in registration fees.

What the ARTL system did, in fact, was increase the time taken for the transaction to be processed; it took longer to deal with online applications than paper forms, defeating the purpose of the electronic system. It was later discontinued.

10. Conclusion

The ARTL is not an isolated incident that an innovation is hailed as revolutionary, expected to improve the workflow and efficiency for lawyers. Still, it actually has the opposite effect. This is perhaps why there can be a tendency towards reticence about adopting and using new systems. But as Accenture noted in their "Six Elements of an Innovation Mindset", the fear of failure, of trying things that might not work, is a key component. Of course, it is preferable that a system is evaluated and tested before millions of pounds are wasted on something that proves ineffective.

Change is a certainty; the law likes dealing in certainty, albeit not always in change! Those firms who actively seek out ways to adopt and improve the innovation mindset in their people, will see the rewards through a host of metrics from increased profits, higher client and staff retention and improved market reputation.

Some coaching questions you can ask yourself about innovation are:

- Where have you seen examples of successful innovation (inside and outside law)? What can you learn from these?
- Where have you noticed attempts at innovation which have not proven successful? Why do you think these failed? What can you glean from this?
- When you consider your favourite brands or service providers you use regularly, what is it about their service that you really like? What can you learn from this?
- As you consider your role/department/team right now, what opportunities for innovation do you see?
- Where is time being wasted, or perhaps tasks being replicated?
- What could be made more efficient in terms of time, money or people power?

Chapter V: Manage your clients

Steve Couch

This chapter offers strategies to evolve your client portfolio. We start by exploring a factor which is typically given less attention yet may be the most influential element in evolving your client portfolio. That factor is you. We then share ideas for understanding your current and future portfolios, before introducing techniques for working with others' perspectives to help you evolve your portfolio. We end the chapter with an examination of the personal and interpersonal skills that may be of greatest value to you now and in the future.

Reading this chapter will give you more ways to answer the questions:*

- How can I build a stronger client portfolio that anticipates future needs?
- To what extent am I working from a fixed mindset rather than a growth mindset?

1. Building more awareness about who you serve, how you serve them and why you serve them

In competitive markets, clients may come and go. At the same time, you may build client relationships that are long lasting, or be at the leading

* In this chapter you will find frequent coaching questions. These are designed to encourage you to pause, reflect and then ponder what you are learning and the impact this could have on you and your future practice.

edge of a short-lived but highly profitable marketing opportunity. What you offer your clients may be relatively constant, meeting predictable needs in long established areas of practice or relatively dynamic, driven by emerging practice in new areas such as genetic modification and cryptocurrency. You may be working with frequent changes in tax law or long-standing precedent in property law.

- Why, today, am I working in these areas of expertise with my client portfolio?

1.1 Working from your perspective

In Chapter I, we examined how knowledge of your changing self and goals informs your continuing professional development. Awareness and understanding of your identity, your motivations, how you work best and your blockers are crucial elements for you to bring your best to your business. Knowing what your clients mean to you and understanding how you want to work with them are also critical factors in how you manage your portfolio.

A first step if you have not considered this before, or recently, is to name your most valuable clients, referred to by some as 'Crown Jewels' clients. Your judgement should be influenced by what you and your business need and not influenced by non-business factors such as friendship.

Financials will be critical for most businesses in this consideration, but should not be your only driver. Market-leading clients may be less profitable, but allow you to do work that can be easily replicated with others. If you are looking for strategic expansion into a new market, geography or segment, an otherwise unremarkable client may be significant in giving you presence.

At the other end of the scale, you might identify the clients that are detrimental to your business, being unprofitable or no longer matched to the way you practise. For example, you may recognise clients that you have outgrown as your practice has developed, or who have outgrown you, for example by becoming more or less internationally focused.

The following exercise may trigger other relevant thoughts:

EXERCISE

Imagine you are holding an award ceremony for your clients. First, identify the awards you want to give, tailoring the award categories to your business and ambition.

Categories might include financial targets such as:

- highest fees;
- most profitable;
- prompt payment; and
- lowest investment in client days (shortest gap between doing work and being paid).

More strategically and subjectively, you could consider:

- most interesting new client;
- highest potential to be a 'Crown Jewels' client;
- best addition to my personal network;
- most technically challenging work;
- work most replicable with other clients; and
- lifetime recognition award.

Next, identify the contenders for each award. Value the clients who sit across several categories. Reconsider those that do not appear and why that is.

What you look for from your client portfolio is likely to change as you work in different ways over time. Consider psychological studies that suggest we look for different things at different life stages. For example, you may recognise these changing motivations as we progress through our careers:

- I want to be recognised.
- I want to be successful.
- I want to be famous.
- I want to be remembered.

These changes can influence the nature of the work that you want to do and the clients that you want to work with at different times in your career.

CASE STUDY – JOSEPH

Joseph is 38 and an established partner. He leads a successful intellectual property practice with an associate and two paralegals. In his early career, as a single man, he gained broad experience working for half a dozen different law firms, regularly moving to new firms to do more interesting and rewarding work. This included two years based in Singapore.

Today Joseph has a young family, a new, larger mortgage, and ambitions for his children to attend fee-paying schools. Contemplating turning 40, he has ambitions to grow his portfolio and build a team in which he can place greater trust.

Joseph wants to spend more time networking with potential clients to generate new work. He is envious of an older colleague who is very active in the local Law Society. At some stage he would like to contribute to Globe Law and Business's book *Intellectual Property Strategy: A Practical Guide to IP Management*.

Joseph has made one successful career transition. He moved from a portfolio most heavily influenced by being recognised for the type of work he did, to a portfolio most influenced by the success he wants to achieve, as seen in a larger house, and family. The future challenge for Joseph is to make a further transition to growing his business; to being more famous.

At this stage, typically entering mid-partnership, it is all too common to see people struggle. Greater financial and relationship commitments, the satisfaction of being established as a partner, and the conviction that no one can do your job as well as you, all argue for not disturbing the *status quo*. Added to these are the day-to-day pressures of meeting ever-changing client demands and market competition. Finally, whereas the earlier paths to recognition and success were relatively clear, there is less clarity on the individual path to fame and legacy.

With all these conflicting factors, it can be easy to lose sight of what you want from your client portfolio. You may be happy to settle for what you have. However, there is a crucial difference between conscious compromise and losing sight of or ignoring what you want.

We see too many professionals who lose track of what they want only to rediscover this later in their career. At this later stage, they realise that the way they worked for success in the past is no longer motivating them and their career progression is stalling.

For example, mid-career loss of motivation may be attributed to the dawning recognition of now being 'stuck in a rut'. Similarly, in later career, the regret of missed opportunities may stem from a sense of having neglected what you wanted to do. Unfortunately, for some this also results in negative mental and physical health consequences.

As we move on to work with client and market perspectives on evolving your portfolio, please continue to give appropriate weight to your own perspective. It is the area over which you have most control not just in evolving your portfolio, but also in fuelling the energy essential to future-proofing success.

- What changes should I plan to my working practices to achieve more of what will motivate me in five years' time?

1.2 Working from your clients' perspectives

- What am I assuming about my client that may no longer be valid?

(a) Working with individual client needs

Your relationships with clients are not static, but dynamic. However, if you bring two or three clients to mind, the mental picture that you have of each client today, may be very similar to the picture you had of them six months – or even five years – ago. Our brains find it easier to recall a relatively dated impression of each client, particularly if this involves strong emotions. Aim for a more current and balanced image.

This is harder. Your brain needs conscious encouragement to think about clients in more questioning and creative ways. Further, this cannot happen at the same time as you are recalling the dated impressions. As you prepare your next meeting, it can be helpful to ask:

- What is different for me, my client and potentially for our working relationship since the last time we engaged?

Seeing the client relationship in this way, as an evolution rather than a constant, can be productive in widening the scope of what you identify in your client. Fresh perspectives can suggest new ways of working, new connections and unearth valuable possibilities for strengthening your client relationships.

It is not always necessary to make educated guesses about how your client views your relationship. Asking them is more effective, but again, your default may too often be what you think you know.

Periodic review meetings provide great opportunities to update yourself on perspectives. You have the chance to update yourself on client perspectives and how they view your relationship. You also have the chance to show your client that you have new thoughts.

- What are the best questions that I can ask my client to increase my awareness of their perspective and our working relationship?

Here are a few that you may find helpful:

- What can I change in our working relationship to make it even stronger?
- What do I think will be different about the way we need to work in the next 12 months?
- How can I help my client to meet/exceed organisational/personal objectives in the next 12 months?

Realistically, you will not be able to do this for every client. Instead, for standard less lucrative work consider identifying client avatars to represent different service offerings.

For your most important clients, distinguishing the perspectives of different organisational stakeholders can create fresh insights about your work with the organisation. For example, an outcome may have little impact on the CFO but could be absolutely critical for your relationships with legal counsel and the CEO. In more complex situations you may want to create a separate perspective for the interests or ethics of the organisation.

- How do I demonstrate to each of my individual clients that I am adapting to meet their individual and organisational needs?

Factors that may influence the nature of each of your client relationships include:

- the size and competence of the in-house law team;
- the organisation's financial performance;
- changes in the organisation's market (eg, disruptive innovation);
- the geography in which the organisation is operating; and
- changes in the regulatory environment.

(b) Working with your creative advisory team (CAT)

As you develop your understanding of different client perspectives, you may also look to increase your range of responses. A straightforward technique to do this involves imagining that you are working with your personal creative advisory team or CAT.

EXERCISE

Creating a CAT starts with you identifying around half a dozen colleagues or role models who operate in different ways. An effective CAT should include people with different working styles, a range of emotions, and people with whose approach you find it difficult to work. For example, you may include John, a cautious colleague; Jane, an innovative colleague; and Jenny, a hard-nosed colleague.

Imagine how various individuals and sub-groups of your CAT would respond in different ways to the client challenges you see.

What do these suggest about how you can enhance your approach?

We may be inclined to think that we have understood our clients and how they work, and that this understanding will not need to change. However, your client relationships will improve if systematically and periodically you examine how, over time, you have changed, your client has changed and what resulting changes are needed to maintain and strengthen your relationships.

(c) Working with evolving organisational needs

Future-proofing your business also means anticipating and understanding the evolving organisational needs of your clients' businesses. This requires keeping up to date with your clients' business strategies and performance, which can be time consuming. A suggestion of how to do this efficiently is to ask yourself:

- Who are the three people most critical for my business with this client that I do not know yet?
- Which three people in my network are the most relevant introductions I can make to this client?

You may also want to ask current client contacts these questions, to create the possibility of your involvement at the early stage of organisational change. For example, being asked to advise on filling an in-house legal team vacancy or recommend an international law firm, can strengthen your understanding of your clients' future business needs.

1.3 Working from both perspectives

In this section we discuss working from a collaborative perspective. We look at insights and opportunities that can be generated by combining your and your clients' perspectives. We also discuss how wider organisational working can strengthen your client relationships. Finally, we look critically at how long you should work with each client.

(a) Strengthening your working relationships

We recommend that you regularly analyse your client portfolio to remind yourself of the relative value to you of each client. You may list your clients in priority order, or identify 'Crown Jewel', 3-star, 2-star and 1-star clients.

In conjunction with this, you can then assess the risk of losing each client before plotting each client on a simple 2x2 grid. We suggest a forced distribution, which might be no more than 30% of your clients in each box:

	Least at risk	Most at risk
Most valuable		(Attend to these first)
Least valuable		

Placing clients in the most valuable–most at risk quadrant will inevitably raise questions about how the risk can be managed. Too often responses look only at what you need to do and overlook the positives and negatives for both parties to the relationship. This is an area where working collaboratively may strengthen relationships.

A first step is to confirm the extent of the risk. If you have not been arranging independent service reviews with the client, it would be wise to do so now to understand and hopefully collaborate on your challenge.

For example, a client's revelation that they are about to ask you to compete for new lucrative work may immediately turn a least valuable into a most valuable asset.

Assuming the risk of potential loss is confirmed, you may consider further questions:

- What can my organisation do that my client is unaware of?
- Which of my colleagues has as good or better relationship than me with this client?

Again, answering these questions can be done in collaboration. Clients may welcome your proactivity more than having to find a new provider.

(b) Why are you working with this client?

Placing clients in the least value–most at risk quadrant raises different questions. As an ambitious professional we suggest that you regularly consider the opportunity costs of working with such clients.

Many practitioners suffer the consequences of postponing client portfolio reviews. Drifting into a position where, for example, 80% of clients by number represent 20% or less of your revenue, can be a strain on your time and on working capital. Reaching this position suggests the need for an unattractive portfolio clean-up exercise.

This raises a provocative question to ask yourself:

- How long should each client relationship last?

Your instinctive answer may be 'forever'. However, there are other plausible responses.

At times you may see your client's business running in parallel with yours, almost complementing one another. At other times the alignment will be less strong. Your client may see this differently and knowing this can be powerful in assessing your relationship.

You have options in how you respond to these changes. A sensible starting point is to consider the boundaries of your current practice and how these may change.

- Which future client needs am I unable to meet currently?
- How do I prepare myself and my client for this?

Depending on the nature of your business, you may prefer to do this in the context of your larger clients, or your most valuable service offerings. For both, proactively addressing differences in the planned future of your business and your understanding of where your client's business is headed offers many benefits. Intangibly these include deepening trust in the relationship and enhancing your reputation. Tangibly, you may find that your understanding of your client's intentions is imperfect, or a way of continuing the work you are doing alongside another specialist provider. Even more powerful can be the development of a collaborative relationship that informs how both parties develop their futures. In this regard, we feel that there is powerful learning in discussing the two coaching questions above with your clients.

Despite all of this, there will be times when you need to discuss ending the working relationship. If you are driving this outcome and your client is unhappy, this may be an opportunity to increase your fee rates. Keep in mind that higher rates offered at this stage may not be sustainable.

Where you are unhappy with this outcome, there are still important collaborative steps you can take to future-proof your career. Providing an introduction to another firm that you know and perhaps with which you already work, takes little time and offers the potential return of future work opportunities for you, either in relation to the individual client or new targets. It is also sensible to recognise that whilst the organisational relationship is ending, there are possibilities that individuals will change jobs and consider you in the future, or simply recommend you to others.

1.4 Working from your competitors' perspectives

The final perspectives to consider are those of your competitors. This may be the most challenging area to work through, likely to involve more assumptions than reflection on your own perspective or exploring your client relationships. Our aims in this section are to help you generate more creative insights about your competitors and then to consider the perspective of new entrants.

(a) Coaching questions

Coaching questions can be particularly powerful in expanding your thinking about your market. The more insights you can reveal about your competitors' future behaviours, the greater the potential for you to take more effective actions in developing your business. The emphasis is not on fearing your competitors' potential, but on increasing your awareness of what is possible for you. The discovery is about what you can do to future-proof your business. Here are some examples.

- What needs are my competitors seeing in my clients that I have yet to notice?

Answering this question can identify client requirements that your competitors are targeting. For example, a payroll organisation may be trying to sell an Employment Law helpline that overlaps with services that you provide. Asking the question from the standpoint of a competitor generates new ideas. You may decide to offer a similar helpline, or to reinforce the quality of your existing services.

- What are my competitors planning to share with my clients that I want them to hear first from me?

This question expands the range of topics about which you can communicate with your clients. As an example, it may be more generative of ideas for your posts and blogs than simply asking: 'What do I want to share with my clients?'

- What do I do that keeps my competitors awake at night?

This question reverses the clichéd consultant question and provides valuable insights into the strength of your business as seen by your competitors. The question works by giving you the opportunity to dissociate yourself from your thoughts and emotions, reducing subjective influences. A similar question of wider application is to ask what you would see if you could look down on your business from above.

(b) Fresh perspectives on competition

Across businesses, there have been significant movements away from traditional markets and growth in disruptive competition in the last 20 years. Professional services organisations have been comparatively resilient to new entrants. This has been due in part to high-entry barriers including necessary knowledge and expertise, and a lack of homogeneity in market requirements. However, it is becoming increasingly clear that larger and more sustainable new business models will emerge. Technological evolution and the related high levels of investment required for significant disruption will be major influences.

From the perspective of larger investors, professional service organisations appear an attractive proposition. Finding cost efficiencies in leadership-heavy firm structures is seen as comparatively straightforward with rainmakers viewed as relatively undervalued in terms of financial investment returns. Further inefficiencies are seen in low levels of collaboration, poor understanding of return on investment and limited use of digital channels to market.

- What will short- and medium-term macro changes mean for my career in the next 10 years?

1.5 Section summary

In this section we have looked at three perspectives on your client portfolio: yours, your clients and your competitors. These are not the only perspectives. You may find it appropriate to consider the perspectives of your practice leadership team, your professional indemnity provider and your staff. Working with these and other perspectives to look at your portfolio from different angles will give you more ideas about the development of your portfolio.

2. Cultivating advanced interpersonal skills

2.1 Why this matters

Increasing importance is being attached to the cultivation of personal skills. For example, in November 2020, the US Securities & Exchange Commission introduced compulsory quarterly disclosure of human capital measures. The measures that organisations now need to disclose include: the percentage of employees who have completed compliance training, total development and training spend, and the percentage of leaders who receive leadership development.

2.2 A growth mindset

Continuous investment in development can no longer be viewed as training for the sake of training. In 2015, intangibles (including an organisation's human capital, intellectual property, etc) represented 84% of the value of the Top 500 quoted US companies, compared to 17%

in 1975.[1] We conclude that regular assessment of your competencies and evidence of what you have done to develop new skills, including leadership skills, will be essential for your future. For most people, this will require increased cultivation of advanced interpersonal skills.

In her book *Mindset* (2017), Carol Dweck highlights the benefits of developing a growth mindset over working with a fixed mindset.[2] She emphasises the benefits of a growth mindset by adding the subtitle *Changing the way you think to fulfil your potential* to the revised edition of her book. The growth mindset involves constant learning, recognition of personal deficiencies, an appetite for taking risks and fostering individual and organisational development.

We hear regularly about established professionals working with a fixed mindset. They are widely seen as unjustifiably complacent, closed to new ways of thinking and out of date. They display unchallenged thinking, pass blame to others, avoid personal reputational risk and look constantly for personal validation. We believe that adopting a growth mindset and being seen to do so are essential to continuing career success, which begs the question:

- How do I demonstrate a growth mindset in my professional life?

There is a continuing need for professionals to cultivate and refresh personal and interpersonal skills. In his book, *To Innovate or Not to Innovate* (2019), Darryl Cooke, founding partner of gunner*cooke* recommends that each of his partners set a weekly target of reading a chapter of a good business book, fully annotating it and recording key soundbites from it.[3] His firm also runs book club meetings where colleagues discuss their learning on contemporary business and behavioural texts.

1 Ocean Tomo LLC, Components of S&P 500 Market Value, 1 January 2015, www.businessintangibles.com/single-post/2015/03/11/intangible-assets-increase-to-84-of-the-sp-500s-value-in-2015-report.

2 Carol S Dweck, *Mindset: Changing The Way You Think to Fulfil Your Potential*, Robinson, 2017.

3 Darryl Cooke, *To Innovate or Not to Innovate: A Blueprint for the Law Firm of the Future*, Globe Law and Business, 2019.

Working with others, like those in the gunner*cooke* book club, can be helpful. Your commitment to others to meet with others makes it more likely that you will do what you plan. The value of a discussion is that it enriches ideas from different personal reflections.

Scheduling group meetings for broader development discussions can also benefit individual discipline to work on personal and interpersonal skills. We advocate group coaching sessions, with a professionally trained group facilitator or coach, as an effective way of increasing individual and group development. This case study, drawn from real-life scenarios, demonstrates the potential benefits.

CASE STUDY – GROUP COACHING FOR EFFECTIVE DELEGATION

During individual annual appraisals a group of partners shared that they were struggling to manage increased client demand and working longer hours. They expressed concerns, to various degrees, about issues that were causing them difficulty including loss of control, poor sleep, decreased motivation and energy, and working weekends rather than spending time with family and friends. The partners agreed to participate in a series of six 90-minute group coaching sessions. Comments and takeaways at the end of each session included:

1st session: "It's good to know it's not just me", "I feel confident to share where I am struggling with this group".

2nd session: "I am beginning to put my feelings about delegation into perspective", "I am going to experiment delegating more work to an associate".

3rd session: "I have started to question whether I should employ someone to help me", "Jane, Mark and I have agreed to form a weekly lunchtime walking group to discuss delegation and other concerns".

4th session: "I am getting more sleep and feel energised", "The best suggestions from the group are now coming from my peers".
5th session: "It was helpful to think about how I can maintain this new way of working", "I did not realise how blinkered I had become in my approach".
6th session: "Delegation is going well", "I am dedicating more time to work on business development", "At the weekend I only work for two hours on Saturday mornings and I don't always need to do this".

2.3 Expanding your listening range

How you listen has a powerful influence on your impact on others, and your personal working efficiency.

Awareness of how you listen, and what you listen to, are important first steps in improving your listening competence. Being able to distinguish the different ways you listen allows you to create a scale to measure how actively you are listening at any time.

EXERCISE

This exercise is designed to help you recognise how you listen at different levels.

Recall a time you listened to music or a podcast using headphones, perhaps on a train or plane journey.

How well were you listening?

Distinguish:

- not hearing;
- simply hearing noise;
- hearing rhythm, or on a podcast, a change of speaker;
- hearing individual instruments or words; and
- singing along to music, or reflecting on the ideas of a podcast.

continued on next page

> Next time you use headphones, try to identify the circumstances when you are listening most intently and when the quality of your listening drops.

Increased familiarity with one's personal listening scale often leads to recognition that listening competency is underused. Many people listen only for the cue of when they can next speak, without reference to what has just been said. Rather than building rapport, doing so can destroy rapport and reduce trust. Conversely, listening to what is being said, before acknowledging, summarising, confirming your understanding and building on it, is highly effective in building stronger relationships and richer collaborative outcomes. Making written notes as you listen results in greater memory retention and reduces inaccuracies.

To listen effectively requires concentration and recognition that listening is hard. Your listening can be strengthened if you listen with the expectation of being surprised, rather than with the assumption of what is about to be said. As we risk becoming increasingly detached in a more complex world, the advantage of more active listening will become more prominent.

2.4 Handling difficult clients and situations

In this section we suggest why we may see more difficult clients and situations in the future, before introducing a five-step approach in section 2.5.

Being able to deal effectively with difficult clients and situations has become an increasingly important attribute for ambitious professionals and our expectation is that this will continue to be the case.

The scope for greater misunderstandings that can fracture client relationships is increasing in a world of increased volatility, uncertainty, complexity and ambiguity (referred to as a VUCA world, see Chapter VII). We are also seeing subversion of shared understanding from the growing use of alternative facts, fake news and augmented reality. Further, with a 2018 survey finding 44% of Generation Z prefer remote rather than face-to-face contact, we can expect more clients to feel rationally upset.[4]

Increases in remote working have seen a major drop in opportunities to informally test understanding, whether with those directly involved or independently. It is harder to avoid ambiguity with comments such as 'Did you really mean to say...?', or 'Was it you that started the discussion about...?', or 'I think that's right and would support you...', or 'That's how I would interpret what she said...'. Our senses will find it harder to gauge strength of feeling and subtlety in what others are saying. All of which means that a constant in working with an apparently difficult client is the need to ensure that you are working with accurate data.

2.5 A five-step model for handling difficult clients

We set out below a five-step process for working with difficult clients. Accurate data is critical at each stage. Each stage starts with a question. The five questions are:

- How am I responding to this?
- What is my best perspective on this?
- How can others help me?
- What can I ask of others including my client?
- How can we resolve this together?

(a) How am I responding to this?

The first step is to be more fully aware of how you are responding and to remind yourself that your brain has evolved three distinct responses to danger. In order, these are:

4 Cancer Research UK, "Millennials shun face-to-face conversations for online chats", 29 January 2018, https://news.cancerresearchuk.org/2018/01/29/millennials-shun-face-to-face-conversations-for-online-chats/.

i) **Instinctive response:** a threat to your person immediately trips the brain into an instinctive unconscious response. This overwhelms other thoughts. For example, if you pick up a very hot plate, you instinctively let go of it before any conscious thought about what you need to do. This thinking originates in the brainstem. Thankfully, unlike some reptiles, our brains have evolved further responses.

ii) **Triggered response:** an incident that is not immediately life threatening, such as a difficult client or the realisation of a personal mistake, generates a reaction in the amygdala, commonly referred to as a flight, fight or freeze response. Here, flight might refer to immediately disengaging from the client, fight to going on the offensive and passionately defending your position and freeze to inaction with the hope that something will turn up. This response will typically feel very powerful. You may have heard of amygdala hijack, a naturally generated anxious response, based on how you feel at this stage. Acting at this stage often results in regret and later retraction.

Table 1: Flight, fight, freeze

Amygdala response	Possible regretful reaction	Possible necessary retraction
Flight	I never want to see that client again	Rebuilding bridges
Fight	I am going to bill them for everything	Reconciliation
Freeze	I'll wait for them to see how valuable I am	Humility

- What is my most commonly triggered response in the face of a difficult client?

There is no single correct response. Learning comes from greater awareness of your response so that you can pause. This is why you may have been advised to take a deep breath before responding. All being well, the final stage will kick in.

iii) **Considered response:** at some stage, and we firmly recommend waiting for it, the executive function of the brain – primarily located in the prefrontal cortex – will respond. As the name suggests, the prefrontal cortex is at the front of the brain and deals with higher functions such as planning, consequences, decision making and judgement. Your amygdala hijack is balanced by a more considered response. You are now ready to move on to step two.

For concise coverage of the neuroscience in this chapter, see *New Scientist* Instant Expert Series, *How Your Brain Works* (2017).[5]

(b) What is my best perspective on this?

The second step is to consider your perspective on the matter and to investigate how you might see matters differently. Again, working with – rather than against – your brain's natural functioning is helpful. Sleep scientists have highlighted the value of balanced sleep in allowing you to use more of your brain's capacity to integrate short- and long-term learning. In common parlance, we often look at things differently after a good night's sleep. It is worth noting that less than seven hours of sleep a night inhibits the brain in performing this valuable function.

You are now at the stage of creating new perspectives about how you reconcile or choose to abandon the situation.

(c) How can others help me?

The third step is to talk to somebody about your situation, perhaps a colleague or coach. This can be a time of high significance. Not seeking help from others, perhaps because you know the answers, or you fear

5 *New Scientist* Instant Expert, *How Your Brain Works: Inside the most complicated object in the known universe*, John Murray Learning, 2017.

losing face, or you don't want to trouble them, can be self-defeating and worse. Experimenting with the words you are planning to use may trigger more appropriate words. Being actively listened to offers assurance and confidence.

(d) What can I ask of others including my client?

Once you are familiar with your best perspective on the difficult client relationships, think again about what you can ask of others. You may want to recall your imaginary team CAT from section 1.2 above. What would they ask? You may now feel that your client is not as difficult as you first thought. Alternatively, you may ask a colleague to act as an intermediary between you and the client. You may identify small changes in your client's behaviour that would reduce your difficulties. For example, strict time allocation of a five-minute summary at the end of each meeting may really help you and make little difference to the client. You might even laugh together about it.

(e) How can we resolve this together?

Finally, take time to define resolution. Avoid the trap of believing that your client is unaware of difficulties and that he/she has had no impact on the change in your relationship. Resolution may not only be about changes in your behaviour. Even if your client is blameless, there could be benefit in sharing with your client that you are trying to change for the benefit of the relationship. Remember, it is likely that your client will feel invested in reducing difficulty in your relationship.

2.6 Section summary

In this section we have set out our case for cultivating your advanced interpersonal skills, discussed ways of doing this and shared ideas about how you can improve the underrated skill of listening. In the final section we looked at using a range of skills to work with challenging clients.

3. Conclusion

In this chapter we have looked at working with different perspectives to increase awareness of how to evolve your client portfolio. This work is underpinned by your perspective and influenced by your colleagues, clients and markets. We have also seen the critical role of a growth mindset in your response to this evolution, and posed coaching questions to broaden your thinking. At the end of the chapter, we focused on techniques to improve listening and handling difficult clients and situations. Reviewing the coaching questions provided in this chapter may trigger new ideas for you now, and in the future.

Chapter VI: Win work

Clare Jones

This chapter explores quotes, bids, pitches and proposals in the context of achieving higher performance in your legal career. How do you get in front of more business opportunities? How do you increase your win rate? How can you create a competitive response to an invitation to tender? How do you best manage pricing and negotiation? What do you do, whether you win or lose?

Winning client work is the end-game for lawyers. You know it matters, yet when you finally get the invitation to pitch, it can also be a poisoned chalice.

Just when you were on top of billing, when your most recent court case was over, you got an invitation to tender. This time, wait for it; you discovered procurement is involved, or the client wanted to create a new legal panel of firms. Are you excited about the opportunity, or are you thinking, 'Here we go again! Life, as I know it, may be over for the next few weeks'?

We have supported veteran Magic Circle firm partners and sole practitioners on numerous pitches across various business sectors over the past 20 years. This work has involved the whole messy business, from informal sales discussions and email quotes to designing and delivering formal contract bids, requests for proposals (RFPs) and detailed tender responses with administration, panel requirements and procurement-proofing. Here we'll refer to all of these variants as 'pitch'.

In truth, we don't recall a lawyer we've ever worked with telling us that they have secretly loved pitching for work and never told us at the time. However, they realise that the sheer effort involved is the culmination of business development effort, it can pay off big time and it is crucial to get it right.

Even providing an email quote can require careful research, positioning and messaging. Unfortunately, this is not a job for colleagues or the marketing department. We, as co-authors agree, you simply cannot outsource your contribution, and you've got to manage, or at least understand and direct, the process.

Whichever your practice area and your win rate, getting better at acquiring clients is a necessary evil in building a long-term legal career. Knowledge is power, and this chapter will tell you what you need to know. Are you ready?

1. How to build an opportunity?

Something happened before that pitch opportunity pinged into your inbox. You spent weeks, months or possibly years creating that opportunity. Even if it came through a referral, you've only been put forward because of the effort you've put in elsewhere. Well done! Just getting to this point is brilliant and testimony to your reputation and resilience.

Opportunity hunting is unpredictable and often exhausting work. It can take years to convert a new contact into a client, yet sometimes further instructions appear out of the blue. You simply never know when you may win a client, so you need a system to trawl for opportunity continually.

Conventional sales wisdom espouses the immense and indisputable value of building deep, trusting client relationships where repeat business and referrals can keep the wolf from the door. However, today's entrepreneurial lawyers have to stoke the fire of opportunity continually. They have to hunt and compete with hungry opponents needing remarkable resilience, vigilance and agility. They feel pressured to be 'on it' at all times, watchful and competent enough to strike and grasp an opportunity when it arises. They have to continually broaden their territory to lead to a long-term flow of clients. They also need to keep clients satisfied, checking in on service delivery to ensure approaching competitors are distant.

Are you happy with the size of your practice? Are you 'settling' and sitting in the comfort zone? You just don't know when one of your clients may choose a competitor or when a contact will leave or move the goalposts, for example creating a legal panel that could erode your revenue or profit. You can do little to control this, but you can build a strategy to quote for and win business. Is it time to upgrade your client acquisition strategy? Don't be a 'Jo Average' lawyer. That's not why you are reading this book. While your current business development techniques may work, are they tired or unambitious? Can you do better? Look at yourself in the mirror. We think you are nodding. Here are three approaches worth having in your gadget kit.

1.1 Stoke the fire of authority

If you start from scratch, look to Chapter IX for some ideas about building your 'thought leader' reputation on social media and other channels. Keep your contacts 'warm' by staying in touch. You need to work out how you are going to build and maintain your growing network. The critical point is to eventually become 'front of mind' when a new opportunity arises.

1.2 Build a referral network

Another option is to develop a referral strategy to leverage your fantastic community of advocates. Every conversation you have is a route to building more relationships. Be brave and ask for introductions. What is the worst thing that can happen? You might want to think about what you can offer in return. Is it time to 'feel the fear and do it anyway'?

1.3 Just ask

It takes work to nurture relationships. You are not aiming to hassle prospects but check in at appropriate intervals to keep the relationship fresh. Equally, don't waste time barking up the wrong tree. You need to 'qualify' (check willingness to buy) the opportunity. There is nothing wrong with asking straight questions at the right time. Just what is the chance for future work, or what is their legal budget? Which firms do they use, and why do they like them? You're not asking for their address or their salary. You are assessing whether and how you may be able to help this prospect in future. Partners we've worked with are often amazed at the positive response they receive.

2. How to be sure this is a promising prospect?

In professional sales jargon, a 'lead' is a person (or organisation) who is a sales prospect. An 'opportunity' is the specific sales deal being pursued, and 'qualification' is the process that uncovers the viability of that lead. Sales top-performers demonstrate the ability to pursue 'qualified leads' more accurately and earlier in the sales process than colleagues. How do they do that?

2.1 Don't chase losers

Have you ever pitched for work only to be rejected with a polite 'no'? It's soul-destroying, but you pick up the pieces and move on. Unfortunately, if things are quiet, feeble opportunities might become more attractive. It's possibly just too tempting to apply the 'not in; can't win' mindset. It's also understandable that a glittering potential opportunity with a stellar brand name or in a hot area of business could potentially seduce the most level-headed lawyer. Perhaps you've too readily cast aside warning signs such as 'I have never met this contact', 'We don't have an office in France', or 'I just don't know which firms we are competing against'.

Not only are the above scenarios flawed justifications for proceeding with a likely loser, but failure can also lead to a negative spin of lost confidence, wasted money and an ongoing saga of frustration and dwindling resource.

It is far easier to say 'no' to weak opportunity if you have other options, hence the value of continually nurturing your pipeline in the first place. You may even impress the prospect by providing good reasons for not pitching. It may even open a conversation about what work you can do for them. Ultimately, to improve your win rate, you have to stop bidding for jobs where you have scant or no chance of success.

2.2 Mark your scorecard

The key to 'qualifying' your sales opportunities is by asking the right questions. At an organisational level, some firms use a sophisticated, weighted model to predict future wins. However, it's possible to create a simple 'bid/no-bid' scorecard. It should indicate if the opportunity is broadly right for you or way off and help more objective decisions. Here is a list of seven essential questions – you can score yourself out of 10 for each:

1. How well does this align with my/my organisation's business goals?
2. Has this prospect been personally recommended to me?
3. How well do I/we know the prospect and their objective/s?
4. To what extent does my/our service meet the RFP requirements?
5. Do I/we know the competitor/s and can I/we win?
6. Can I/we deliver a fee that can win and make a profit?
7. Can I/we deliver a winning pitch document with all information required on time?

With a maximum mark of 70, what does your estimated score tell you? Should you bid or not bid on this occasion?

It may also help to reconsider previous attempts to win work, whether lost or won. Hindsight is an easy thing, but you may shed some light on why you won or lost by asking these questions again. You may even see some patterns. For example, suppose you do not have a strong existing relationship with the company or individual inviting you to pitch (or a personal referral or recommendation). In that case, it is going to be virtually impossible to succeed.

3. How to put your best foot forward?

CASE STUDY

ABC Ltd *is a national, acquisitive business with a property portfolio, thousands of staff and litigation culture. Potential fees run into hundreds of thousands, and if disputes get out of control, possibly more. The new head of legal isn't happy with the incumbent law firm and invited two law firms recommended to respond to an RFP with a 14-day deadline.*

Partner A of Firm A was pleased to be invited to pitch. *He vaguely knew the head of legal and, two days before the pitch flung together a few credentials in a document. A few hours before the pitch deadline, he contacted the marketing department, asking them to 'jazz it up'. ABC is a big business, so he pitched at his top hourly rate. He seemed incredibly proud of having prepared his submission so quickly. Off it went one minute before the deadline.*

Partner B of Firm B also received an invitation. *She was busy advising on a merger but replied immediately to arrange a 'discovery call'. She also set aside time to work on the pitch for the next two weeks. She approached the marketing team early. On the discovery call with ABC, she uncovered complex organisational politics and some 'hot'* *issues not mentioned in the pitch. She learned about the head of legal's role and budgeting process. She produced an insightful, strategically priced, professionally designed response to the RFP, which was sent in good time.*

Reflections

- Which firm demonstrated hunger, collaboration and trust?
- Which firm would you hire?
- Which partner are you?

3.1 Focus on the goal

You've decided to go ahead and pitch. So, what are you (and the prospect) trying to accomplish? Be clear about your goals and strategy and get to work. In his book *The Elegant Pitch* (2016),[1] author Mike Figliuolo suggests you think first about your communication goal, your audience's goals and the best way to put forward your case.

Forensically review the RFP document (or the brief, however informal). Instructions around the length and format of the response should tell you all you need to know, including the preferred response content and structure and how you will be evaluated and scored. It may be time for a highlighter pen and a notebook, or even a spreadsheet. Then reread the RFP.

You'll need to consider some questions:

- What is the core need here and what problems need solving?
- Where is the opportunity and challenge arising in this business sector?
- What is my/our clear value proposition (including added value investment)?

1 Mike Figliuolo, *The Elegant Pitch*, Career Press, 2016.

- Do I/we offer the right fit/personal 'chemistry'/skills and ideas?
- What case studies come to mind that can showcase relevant experience?
- Who are my/our competitors, and how do I/we need to tweak my/our offer?
- What are the risks of hiring me/us, and how can I/we minimise those risks?
- What are the requirements/deadlines, and can I/we meet these?
- What questions do I/we have (eg, who decides? How does scoring work? Why are you changing provider?)?

3.2 Plan to win

The key to success for all types of submission is a robust process to increase the efficiency and effectiveness of your bid. You will need a solid project plan to meet the deadline. Ideally, you'll build in some contingency. 'One minute before deadline' submissions are life-shortening for everyone involved, so allow contingency time to refine and proofread your bid.

3.3 Use tools and systems

Unless you are a sole practitioner or do not have access to a marketing department or pitch consultancy, you will get help drafting your pitch. You may have IT systems to capture and measure your sales pipeline and report on previous pitch success. You will probably have access to a range of tools across the pitch process, including a well-stocked bid library. A suite of templates will be invaluable in developing a first draft 'skeleton' document.

Otherwise, you will have your work cut out for you, especially if you respond to a formal pitch. Suppose you are going to be pitching for work regularly as a solo legal entrepreneur. In that case, it's time to start thinking about building a suite of generic boilerplates and creating a system to help you plan, price and write your proposal.

3.4 Write to engage

You are most likely to be expected to follow your brand guidelines, but remember this document is not about you or your firm. Therefore, you'll want to use structure, design, language and tone appropriate and aligned to the client opportunity. In his book *Pitch Anything* (2011), author Oren Klaff cites neuroscience. He tells us that we need to impress the reptilian part of the human brain, responding to information at a basic emotional level. To do so, he recommends we make our pitch quickly understood and presented in a logical, intuitive way.[2]

Here are our top writing tips:

- Bash out the first draft fast so you can focus on creating core value.
- Do not be tempted to copy and paste; your work should be unique.
- Follow a logical structure and ensure plenty of time (to enlist a non-lawyer) for proofreading.
- Eliminate jargon and use accessible language, especially if you're a more 'nerdy' lawyer in a highly technical area. In her TED talk (2012), Melissa Marshall explains that you need to share ideas in non-technical terms.[3]
- Tailor your content. Use *relevant* case studies, testimonials, anecdotes and examples. Add detailed, considered and generous exploration of your target client's issues or strategic options.
- Use images that are appropriate to their business and not yours.
- If there are appendices, make sure they are clearly labelled and presented in a sensible order.
- Include a personalised cover letter highlighting the key benefits you offer.

2 Oren Klaff, *Pitch Anything: An Innovative Method for Presenting, Persuading and Winning the Deal*, McGraw-Hill, 2011.

3 Melissa Marshall, "Talk Nerdy to Me", TED talk (2012), www.ted.com/talks/melissa_marshall_talk_nerdy_to_me/up-next.

3.5 Create absolute value

According to author Jill Konrath in her book, *Irresistible Value Propositions* (2012), potential clients should be able to clearly articulate what you might offer their business.[4] She argues that your value proposition needs to state the measurable and quantifiable business value your services offer. Focus on results: increased revenue, improved customer retention, and so on.

Put your energy into the research. You may need to set up a 'discovery call' with the prospect to ask further questions and seek clarifications. Use your findings to think creatively, come up with ideas, share legal insight and make recommendations.

In his TED talk (2007),[5] David Rose, a self-described 'serial entrepreneur' who has raised millions of dollars, states presentations are an "emotional journey" for the audience. He recommends "beginning dramatically, making your case logically and ending powerfully". Rose talks about the value of storytelling and even guides you to identify your competition and clarify what sets your firm apart. Whilst this may be a bold, if not inappropriate, strategy for you, this is food for thought.

In *The Elegant Pitch* (2016),[6] Mike Figliuolo recommends having a thoroughly thought through strategy so you don't spend time researching the wrong issues. Focus first on your suggested solution, then explain the rationale for your advice and finally outline what implementation is needed. This "hypothesis-driven" system relies on facts and data. And it will assist you in delivering clear, compelling information. Figliuolo particularly warns against "confirmation bias", which can arise if you focus only on data that support your case.

3.6 Minimise talking about yourself

Chapter II of this book explains the trustworthiness and authenticity that comes from prioritising our prospect's needs. When responding to

4 Jill Konrath, *Irresistible Value Propositions*, e-book, JillKonrath.com, 2012.
5 David Rose, TED talk (2007), www.ted.com/talks/david_s_rose_how_to_pitch_to_a_vc/up-next.
6 Mike Figliuolo, *The Elegant Pitch*, Career Press, 2016.

invitations to pitch, it is time to step into your prospect's shoes, get excited about their business or, possibly, 'feel their pain'. Don't be disconnected or unadventurous – it's an opportunity to differentiate your services and sell its benefits (to your prospect), not features.

Marketing consultant Andy Raskin of presentation software firm Zuora introduces the elements that make up their "epic" narrative structure in sales pitches by recommending that you don't begin a sales discussion by droning on about yourself. You need to, instead, highlight the big issues that will impact on your prospect and therefore lead to your solution.[7]

It's also perfectly reasonable to justify that you are the best choice, as long as your claims have evidence. Ideally, you'll use case studies and testimonials to validate your offering.

3.7 Be brave with design

Every pitch needs to look professional, so do the basic housekeeping to ensure consistency around the font used and that the layout includes plenty of 'white space' and uses diagrams, images, bullet points and lists.

Want to go the extra mile? We've seen video pitches, professional photography included of the whole team outside one of the target's offices (including a dog!), a proposal delivered on a memory stick in a popcorn container and all manner of creative solutions. Ad agencies are gurus of the off-the-wall pitches, which, to be fair, are more typical in that industry.

Whether you see such tactics as overly keen (desperate), unnecessary or excitingly creative, you need to think about the appropriateness and return on investment in your case. If your prospect wants a short email quote, deliver that. If you've decided your pitch needs to be more creative, don't be lazy. Here's where designers and marketers can be of immense value.

7 Andy Raskin, "The Greatest Sales Deck I've Ever Seen", 15 September 2016, https://medium.com/the-mission/the-greatest-sales-deck-ive-ever-seen-4f4ef3391ba0.

4. How to price to win and make a profit?

Pricing is core to every pitch, whether you're a partner in a global firm or a solo legal entrepreneur. You may be offering a simple email quote or delivering a complex tender document, but every prospect expects a fee.

THOUGHT LEADERSHIP

*We interviewed **David Abbott**, the international pricing expert, and asked him for practical tips on how lawyers can price to win and grow their business. Based on his own vast industry experience, his advice to many lawyers and other professionals is based on behavioural science research.*

Establish value

All pricing should start with clarity around value. Otherwise, you're just offering a commodity where the lowest price wins. 'Value' is so much more than only a number and non-financial elements are core, for example:

- The business might aim to sell. Although financial value is significant, the management team left behind wants to start with a strong standing.
- A commercial contract might be important in terms of revenue but it may also be the key to a board promotion.
- In an employment tribunal over unfair dismissal, the employer has a burning desire to be vindicated.

A decision on the choice of an adviser is influenced by how much the prospect feels they and their goals are understood. Dig beneath the surface and find the clues. It's not about you; it's usually about them.

Decide on the fee

You now need to decide on the fee you will propose, so ask yourself these questions:

- What is the 'going rate' (baseline) in the market?
- Do you specialise in a particularly arcane part of the law where the prospect's choice is limited?
- What is your brand in the market? How much does the prospect want you?
- How badly does the prospect need your specific services?
- Are there any exceptional circumstances? For example, does the job need to be handled quickly? Do you have a relationship with a third party that can overcome obstacles? Or can you be flexible with your time and availability?
- What is the state of the economy and business climate?
- Are there any rules or regulations that are relevant?

Use your judgement to calculate a fee. If the hourly rate or fixed fee seems too high and you are concerned it will be rejected by the client, you are likely to not be alone.

Rehearse

Your potential client wants and expects you to talk about money, yet most of us lack confidence and fear rejection on this subject. As daft as it may seem, practise speaking your fees out loud in front of a mirror. Or enlist supportive colleagues or friends to endorse your value.

Negotiate and communicate

You are clear about your value and fee, so you must be ready for an amicable, breezy, reasonable negotiation with the prospect saying 'yes'? Unfortunately, it isn't always so simple. However, you can improve your likelihood of success with four presentation techniques.

Offer more than one solution

Look for ways to enhance rather than discount your fee. If the prospect wants XYZ, think about what they might not have considered and offer XYZ plus. Try to find at least three options. The evidence is that when presented with a price, prospects tend to make an instant decision, whether that price is fair. When they receive your fee proposal, prospects will subconsciously compare your price with previous, competing, similar or alternative services. By providing them with a choice, you steer that price comparison to within your service offering, not outside of it. For instance, a prospect might want you to represent them in an employment tribunal. You can offer the price for that; the price for a tribunal, a review of their employment contracts and handbook; and a tribunal, contract review and some management training.

Order pricing strategically

If you are going to offer more than one price, the highest goes first. Don't offer three options which are £15,000, £18,000 and £21,000, instead offer £21,000, £18,000 and £15,000. That's because people anchor on the first number they see and compare the rest of what they see to that. So £18,000 and £21,000 look expensive compared to £15,000, while £18,000 and £15,000 look cheap compared to £21,000. Even better, create an anchor by talking about the value you will deliver:

- The £10,000,000 contract you helped to win.
- The £1,000,000 risk your advice averted.
- The £100,000 profit clients make on average, then mention your fees.

Be precise

If you think the job will take 12 hours and you usually charge £250 p/h, the fee will be £3,000. However, whether you offer a fixed price or quote the hourly rate, both seem suspiciously round. The prospect subconsciously ponders, "why £250 p/h or why £3,000?" Interestingly, precise numbers, such as £263 p/h or £3,156, create the sense that there is some rigour involved. The evidence also shows that exact numbers tend to get negotiated down less than round numbers.

Negotiate discounts

Finally, if you enter a negotiation with a prospect, don't merely agree to a concession but request something in return: "Sure, I could do it for £200 p/h, but in return, I'd like a personal introduction to these three companies I know you are connected to."

5. What next?

That moment when you've pressed the send button or sealed the envelope (in good time for the deadline) is sublime. Or is it? You can do very little now but wait. You might begin to relive every paragraph and scrutinise your efforts against your competitors. So apart from exercising some deep breathing techniques, what happens now?

5.1 Be ready for a presentation or interview

Depending on the formality and value of your pitch, there may be a further stage before the outcome. You might be asked to present alone or with your team. Equally, your prospect may wish to conduct interviews with shortlisted suppliers to clarify certain aspects of tenders and take a view on the elusive 'chemistry'. Cue the awkward moment where you meet your arch-rival in the reception area of your prospect's office.

The good news is that you've been shortlisted, and you're still in the game. However, these situations are challenging and how you conduct yourself at this stage requires consideration:

- Who else is on the shortlist?
- Do you need to produce additional materials?
- Who will be at the meeting?
- What questions might be asked?
- What do you need to know more about and ask?
- Who can/should attend from your team?

A presentation or interview is a second chance to showcase your best side, and we recommend a 'dry run' to practise with your team. In the larger firms, it's common to use actors to pose as interviewers, so feel free to pull out all the stops if it is worth it. It's all about the potential return on investment.

5.2 Accept the result

Eventually, you'll face one of two outcomes, both of which require further actions on your part. There can only be one winner.

(a) Outcome 1: You're the winner. Hurrah!

Remember that no one scores full marks, and there are always lessons to learn. Of course, you will soon become busy onboarding your new client and getting to work on the project. Do also consider how you might impress them with a review meeting on any aspects of your bid that did not meet standards or in setting new key performance indicators (KPIs). And if you have a broader conversation about their experience of the pitch process, you may even be able to glean some valuable competitive insights.

(b) Outcome 2: Unfortunately, you lost this time. Sorry!

Sadly, this unwelcome news happens, but taking the time to learn why you failed and what you can do next time separates the good from the great. If you feel this was unfair and that you should have won, you could always take a Trumpian stance and challenge the decision. A Big 4 accountancy firm allegedly based their global pitch guidance around a theme of 'refuse to lose' and worked with partners on how to challenge an unfavourable outcome. Whatever your view, your energy would be well spent on securing a debrief to help you to understand where you went wrong, as well as to define your perceived strengths.

5.3 Get feedback

Getting honest feedback is usually more comfortable if you use a third party, perhaps a senior colleague or independent interviewer. While it's entirely possible to seek electronic feedback, there's nothing better than a phone call to elicit the gruesome detail and probe in particular areas. You don't want to subject a busy prospect to a lengthy Spanish inquisition, so ensure the conversation is focused on these critical areas:

- Who won, and what was the strength of that submission?
- How many pitches were received, and where did yours rank?
- What was the winning score, and what was your score?
- Were there any criteria where you didn't meet the standard?
- What areas of your pitch can be improved?

Equipped with the information, you should have a clearer understanding of why your pitch was unsuccessful and some valuable insights. The feedback should be shared internally within your organisation to raise issues and develop and implement plans to address shortcomings. Hopefully, the reward of the exercise is a more substantial and more compelling pitch next time around.

6. Conclusion

Now it's time to be accountable to your new pitch guru: you!

What are your key action points from reading this chapter? Here are 10 coaching questions to ask yourself right now. Feel free to add more.

1. What am I doing on a daily basis to build my network?
2. What is the first thing I need to do to improve my sales hustle?
3. How can I better communicate with prospects in future?
4. How do I ensure I qualify opportunities and not waste effort with the wrong prospects in the longer term?
5. How am I ensuring I have a competitive value proposition?
6. What is my pricing strategy?
7. What systems and processes do I have to help me to win work?
8. How could I improve these to help me to win work?
9. What can I do to better learn from pitches I win and lose?
10. What do I need to do to ensure I keep my clients and gain referrals?

Pitches, bids, proposals or whatever you prefer to call them are not for your marketing department to win and they're the culmination of years of your hard work in cultivating your business relationships. You owe it to yourself to master them. It's tricky for anyone else to know what it is that will make you win. You know your value. And you should know your prospect. If you don't take responsibility for your ultimate success, who should? It's a job to be done and number six of the essential career-building tools that will serve you well moving ahead. Good luck. Enjoy winning work. May you be noticed, preferred and chosen!

Chapter VII: Lead effectively

Steve Couch

We are rapidly understanding more about the extent to which leaders are born or made, a subset of the wider nature vs nurture debate. For example, we know now that the potential for our brains to wire and rewire is not restricted to childhood years. As a leader, your brain has the capacity to reorganise and grow (neuroplasticity) in response to factors including working in new environments and repetition of desired behaviours. Other studies of the brain have revealed more about how we can learn more effectively, allowing richer insights on how to nurture your leadership approach.

Current thinking suggests that as a leader, you are roughly one-third born and two-thirds made. In other words, you have the capacity to improve your leadership effectiveness by adopting new inherent and new learned leadership behaviours.

This chapter provides insights on contemporary leadership practices and suggests how you can develop to meet future expectations of leadership. We will cover:

- what influences changes in leadership approaches;
- contemporary leadership approaches;
- your strength portfolio; and
- how new leadership approaches will emerge.*

* In this chapter you will find frequent coaching questions. These are designed to encourage you to pause, reflect and then ponder what you are learning and the impact this could have on you and your future practice.

By the end of this chapter, you will have covered material to inform how you answer questions including:

- How do I adapt my leadership approach to appropriately match changing circumstances?
- How do I future-proof the way I lead?

1. What has influenced leadership approaches?

1.1 Recent historical context

Historically, approaches to leadership practice and development have concentrated on the qualities needed to perform the leadership role. Leadership development has leaned towards identifying and evolving the specific skills required for successful leadership. Until relatively recently, leadership development in professional services firms concentrated on strengthening weaknesses, in the hope that over time leaders would develop a full portfolio of skills. Leadership assessment tools were designed so that recognition of strengths was automatically matched with weaknesses. Rather than deploying partners to areas where they could use their strengths to make a difference, it was commonplace for partners to be allocated responsibilities in 'areas for improvement'.

There were negative consequences with this approach. First, the organisation was likely to underperform whilst various partners learned from their mistakes. Secondly, partners were likely to be demotivated by spending more time doing what they disliked and less time doing what they liked. Thirdly, the practice reinforced leadership approaches which resort to exposure of others' weaknesses as a way to feel superior.

For practices that have retained elements of this approach, it may be helpful to ask:

- As a leader, how often do I praise my colleagues' strengths?

In *Go Put Your Strengths to Work* (2007), Marcus Buckingham asked "Is finding your weaknesses and fixing them the best way to achieve outstanding performance?"[1] This question is still worth asking today.

1 M Buckingham, *Go Put Your Strengths to Work*, Simon & Schuster, 2007, p40.

A more powerful leadership question emerges from switching the words around and asking:

- What is the best way for you to achieve outstanding performance by finding and deploying your leadership strengths?

But as weaknesses could be an obstacle to achieving outstanding performance, a further question is needed:

- Who can help me to compensate for my leadership weaknesses?

These questions bring into sharp focus the importance of self-awareness as a leader. We will discuss this further in section 3. Before that, in the rest of this section we examine what underlies new requirements of leadership, and in section 2 leadership approaches that have been developed in response.

1.2 What has changed?

In the last 30 years there have been significant changes in what we expect of leadership. Increasing role demands mean that traditional single person leadership, what Manfred Kets de Vries described as "super-hero" leadership,[2] is an unrealistic expectation of any human. In *Team of Teams* (2015), General Stanley McChrystal sums this up succinctly saying:

> *We expect our leaders to know everything, knowing full well that the limits of technology and the human brain won't allow it.*[3]

We can illustrate what is commonly described as cognitive overload from different perspectives.

(a) Broader risk management

The Global Risks Report[4] which is published annually by The World Economic Forum captures CEOs' views about the risks they face. Five categories of risk are used to describe the nature of these risks: economic, environmental, geopolitical, societal and technological. The contrast

2 M Kets de Vries, *The Hedgehog Effect: The Secrets of Building High Performance Teams*, Jossey-Bass, 2011, p56.

3 S McChrystal, *Team of Teams: New Rules of Engagement in a Complex World*, Penguin, 2015, p222.

4 World Economic Forum, *The Global Risks Report 2021*, www.weforum.org/reports/the-global-risks-report-2021.

Table 1: Top five global risks in terms of impact

	2021		2012	
	Specific risk	Risk category	Specific risk	Risk category
1	Infectious diseases	Societal	Major systemic fiscal failure	Economic
2	Climate action failure	Environmental	Water supply crises	Societal
3	Weapons of mass destruction	Geopolitical	Food shortage crises	Societal
4	Biodiversity loss	Environmental	Chronic fiscal imbalances	Economic
5	Natural resource crises	Environmental	Energy and agricultural price volatility	Economic

between the top five risks for 2021 and 2012 in Table 1 demonstrate change and the increasing complexity of risks that leaders face. Whereas in 2012 leaders could address the risk factors from a largely internal perspective (three probably sat with the CFO), the 2021 risk factors cover more risk categories and require more leadership time and broader knowledge.

(b) Data

In *The Organized Mind* (2015), Daniel Levitin reported that in 2011 Americans were taking in five times as much information every day as they did in 1986 – the equivalent of 175 newspapers. He suggested the processing power of the brain is limited to the equivalent of 120 bits a day.[5] Demand is greater.

(c) Loss of concentration

In addition, your brain finds it difficult to separate the trivial from the necessary. This can be seen on a scale ranging from spending too much

5 D Levitin, *The Organized Mind*, Penguin, 2014, p6.

time listening to your inner critic or being drawn in by clickbait. We behave this way because we enjoy the immediate benefits. For example, the positive impact of giving or receiving a 'like' engages reward neural pathways, offering a shot of dopamine, a chemical that contributes to feelings of alertness, motivation and happiness. The downside is the contribution this makes to cognitive overload.

- How do I continuously create the space needed to avoid cognitive overload?

1.3 A VUCA world

The acronym VUCA represents volatility, uncertainty, complexity and ambiguity. First used in the context of modern warfare during the 1990s, VUCA has become commonplace as a term to describe the unpredictable global business environment.

For example, increasing volatility is seen in the changing nature of competitive threat and shortened product life cycles that necessitate frequent refinement of operating models.

The lack of clarity about potential future variants of COVID and the imposition of further lockdowns are the most vivid examples of business uncertainty.

Increasing complexity is seen in the explosion of data, with estimates that the amount of data in the world doubles approximately every 13 months.

Ambiguity and misunderstanding are seen in the increase in cross-cultural perspectives and challenges to social structures and hegemonies. For example, differences in enduring cultural expectations of leadership are increasingly visible internationally. In some cultures, the leader will command the necessary respect due to status; in other cultures, emphasis is placed on delivering results and the charisma of the leader.

1.4 Section summary

In this section we have examined the shortfalls of traditional leadership approaches and discussed why these are incongruent with future leadership requirements. Meeting the challenges of a VUCA world requires more collaborative ways of working which we will cover in the next chapter. Before that, in the next section, we explore contemporary leadership approaches that have been developed for more effective leadership, now and in the future.

2. Contemporary leadership approaches

2.1 Introduction

There have been significant changes in the job specification for professional service firm leadership. In recent memory, senior partners were regarded as partly figurehead, credible because of their extensive practice experience and high-standing in their profession, and partly as commanders of high respect from their colleagues for what they had contributed to their practice. For many, the role was the pinnacle of a highly successful career. However, the role was also consciously avoided by talented practitioners, keen to remain in their practice area. Many were uninspired by the role's increasingly unattractive requirements, which included the need to develop a new portfolio of skills, for which most of the training was through trial and error on the job. Discussions of how to professionalise the senior partner role became more common whenever partners gathered.

In this section we consider a range of leadership approaches that have emerged in recent years.

2.2 What has changed

The mindset for electing a senior leader has changed. It is no longer a question of who is most deserving of recognition in the role. Instead, the first questions that may be asked are:

- Where are we, where do we want to go and who is best placed to lead us there?

Once these have been identified, a choice can be made based on the candidates' capabilities in these areas.

In recent times absences of specific capabilities have been reported as contributing to significant senior resignations. These offer guidance on contemporary leadership qualities. Examples include knowing when to consult others, displaying emotional intelligence and knowing exactly how much of the future can be introduced into the present.

The emphasis on leadership's ability to respond to change can be traced back to the initial development of models of situational leadership in the 1970s and 1980s. Situational leadership was based on the idea that different styles of leadership were needed depending on where the organisation was in the business cycle. At different stages, businesses' requirements could be best met by visionary, practical, motivating and disruptive leaders.

More recently, an offshoot of situational leadership has grown and is now of equal importance. This is the need to motivate and inspire people to engage, whether as fellow leaders, employees, clients, stakeholders, influencers or the wider world.

The unpredictability of future situations also makes it critical for leaders to build succession by growing a pool of potential leaders covering a broad spectrum of future capability requirements.

In the rest of this section we look at four models of leadership that have emerged more recently. We do this not to recommend a model that you should work with; as we do not know your situation, we cannot do this. Our aim is to encourage you to reflect regularly on the situations in which you find yourself and the leadership approaches you adopt.

2.3 Authentic pragmatism

In the title of their 2006 book, Rob Goffee and Gareth Jones asked leaders to reflect on a question that remains pertinent now: "Why should anyone be led by you?"[6]

Their answer to this question was that leaders need to be authentic, which in turn required greater self-knowledge. Leadership requires consistency which can only be maintained if you are true to yourself.

6 R Goffee and G Jones, *Why Should Anyone Be Led By You?*, Harvard Business Review Press, 2006.

Goffee and Jones recognised the need to be pragmatic as well as authentic with chapter headings such as: "Be Yourself – More – with Skill", "Remain Authentic – but Conform Enough", "Communicate – with Care" and "Know and Show Yourself – Enough".[7]

Authentic pragmatism exemplifies approaches that emphasise the importance of leading with emotional intelligence, a concept embracing your personal motivation, self-awareness, self-regulation, enhanced social skills and empathy. It is leadership that is less concerned with status and power and more interested in empowering others to own and drive desired outcomes. It is leadership that is self-disciplined and consistent, conscious of what leaders represent and demonstrative about role modelling behaviours.

Authentic pragmatism is of relevance because of the chord it appears to strike with millennials. For the first time in 2020, over 50% of the global workforce was millennial.[8] New Zealand's Jacinda Ardern, viewed as a favourite leader by millennials, described her leadership approach as:

> *Kindness, and not being afraid to be kind, or to focus on, or be really driven by empathy… because we've placed over time so much emphasis on notions of assertiveness and strength – that we probably have assumed that it means you can't have those other qualities of kindness and empathy.*
>
> *And yet, when you think about all the big challenges that we face in the world, that's probably the quality we need the most. We need our leaders to be able to empathise with the circumstances of others; to empathise with the next generation that we're making decisions on behalf of.*
>
> *And if we focus only on being seen to be the strongest, most powerful person in the room, then I think we lose what we're meant to be here for.*

7 *Ibid.*
8 PwC (2018), "Workforce of the future: The competing forces shaping 2030", www.pwc.com/gx/en/services/people-organisation/publications/workforce-of-the-future.html.

So I'm proudly focused on empathy, because you can be both empathetic and strong.[9]

Playing up your natural empathy and playing down contradictory behaviours will demonstrate authentic pragmatism.

- When did I last feel inauthentic and why did this happen?

2.4 Charismatic connector

The charismatic connector leadership perspective emerged out of a 2012 symposium on the requirements of contemporary leadership. The approach emphasises personal relatability and exploration of organisational potential, founded on the idea that greater organisational capability is discoverable. It can be seen as a continuous search for the extra pieces of an ever-expanding strategic jigsaw puzzle.

Being a charismatic connector involves understanding the edge of networks, and asking questions to identify what is possible informed by new perspectives that others offer. There is less focus on individual capabilities and more on collective capabilities that can best be realised by focusing on what is possible in the space between individuals. This perspective may be particularly relevant for law firms which struggle to break down silos.

The charismatic element builds and then strengthens relationships. This builds the trust needed to realise more of what is possible. Charisma acts as an inspirational glue to join people together.

Elements of charisma are being able to put others at ease and, crucially, inspiring others to be more confident in what they can do. Leaders with charisma role model openness to learning, ask questions and show genuine interest in answers. This is generative and allows for greater individual connections across an organisation.

9 Geoff Blackwell, "Jacinda Ardern: 'Political leaders can be both empathetic and strong'", *The Guardian*, 30 May 2020, www.theguardian.com/world/2020/may/31/jacinda-ardern-political-leaders-can-be-both-empathetic-and-strong.

Connectivity also involves seeking ideas from inside and outside your organisation and acknowledging temporary weaknesses so that in time you can increase your influence and impact.

- How can I incorporate the charismatic connector model into my leadership approach?

2.5 Team of teams

In *Team of Teams: New Rules of Engagement in a Complex World* (2015),[10] General Stanley McChrystal applies his experiences of commanding military task forces in Iraq and Afghanistan to organisational leadership. As a commander, McChrystal learned that the power of superior troop numbers and weaponry were insufficient to achieve successful outcomes. Traditional warfare responses were ineffective, in the face of unstructured and complex opposition tactics. They were flawed because they relied on factors including long chains of command, detailed analysis, asynchronistic communication and micromanagement.

McChrystal chose not to see leadership as the role of "the Great Man or the Great Woman" (Bennis).[11] Instead, he approached his function with the aim of creating sufficient trust and connectivity to provide unprecedented levels of organisational knowledge, to those who needed it to act decisively. In 2006, the impact of this change in leadership approach was to increase the number of raids per month from eighteen to three hundred.

These practices drawn from *Team of Teams* are applicable to professional services:

(a) Building trust and connectivity

Treat trust and connectivity as the bedrock of your leadership practice. Look to build leadership trust as a reciprocal process, recognising that

10 S McChrystal, *Team of Teams: New Rules of Engagement in a Complex World*, Penguin, 2015.
11 W Bennis, *Four traits of leadership. The Leader vs. Manager: Their Existence*, 1986, pp79–89.

others' trust in you and your trust in others are essential for higher levels of performance.

One of the consequences of increased home working during COVID lockdown has been the increase in employee monitoring. In January 2021, *Personnel Today* reported a YouGov poll that found that one in five firms were implementing or planning to introduce "secret software used to spy on staff".[12]

The potential value of monitoring should be weighed against the impact of higher levels of employee mistrust.

- What do I do regularly to demonstrate my trust in those around me?

(b) Adapt to rapidly changing situations

McChrystal learned to work with the uncertainty of not knowing all the facts. He recognised a trait of leaders to over involve themselves in decision making for the wrong reasons:

> *Being woken to make life-or-death decisions confirmed my role as a leader and made me feel important and needed... I could ask thoughtful questions but I had no illusion that my judgment was markedly superior to the people with whom I worked.*[13]

Opportunities could vanish during the time taken to cover off every single 'what if', and to hand responsibility for every specific task to the leader.

We can see parallels with McChrystal's suggestion to adapt rapidly in changing situations in professional practice. For example, once upon a time, every handwritten letter an associate drafted was first reviewed by a senior, and, eventually after a potential series of redrafts, handed up to a partner who would send it down and up the chain as many times as necessary for subjective perfection.

12 Richard Fox and Eleanor Lynch, "Employee surveillance: getting the balance right", *Personnel Today*, 22 January 2021, www.personneltoday.com/hr/employee-surveillance-getting-the-balance-right/.

13 S McChrystal, *Team of Teams: New Rules of Engagement in a Complex World*, Penguin, 2015, p202.

- If this practice seems ridiculous to you, what current practices in your organisation might look similarly ridiculous in a few years' time?

In practice, leaders need to achieve greater flexibility by developing organisational culture that reflects principles, rather than dip into detail. In his time as PwC senior partner, Sir Ian Powell offered a powerful example of this, reinforcing the message that his partners shared leadership responsibility by constantly asking them to "do the right thing".[14]

- What are the limiting factors of my leadership that I have not addressed?

There is great scope to increase the roles of governance and organisational culture to contribute to organisational effectiveness. For example, rather than seeing governance as a tick-box exercise it is worth considering the beneficial role it can play in supporting how employees behave in unfamiliar situations.

- How can I make more use of governance training and organisational culture to engender greater behavioural certainty in my organisation?

Making more of governance and organisational culture will contribute to what McChrystal described as a "eyes on, hands off",[15] which is appropriate for greater organisational flexibility.

2.6 Paradoxical leadership

Our final model is the evolving approach of paradoxical leadership. As you might guess, leading with paradox brings apparent contradictions to the fore.

Where previously leaders may have been encouraged to show consistency in their approach, leading with paradox suggests an

14 Sir Ian Clifford Powell, personal communication.

15 S McChrystal, *Team of Teams: New Rules of Engagement in a Complex World*, Penguin, 2015, p218.

expansive mindset that is comfortable with apparently contradictory responses resulting from situational nuances. In McChrystal's words: "... the idea that a problem has different solutions on different days."[16]

Paradoxical leadership has been described as a shift from 'either/or' leadership to 'both/and' leadership where apparently contradictory ideas are accommodated. Decision making has evolved from choosing between different options and then maintaining consistency with that choice. Instead, the approach is to see how apparently contradictory positions can be maintained at the same time, a best of both worlds approach.

For example, in the past, a decision may have been made for leaders to focus on overseas expansion, at the expense of what was needed domestically. The question which may have been asked is: 'How does what we do in our domestic business apply to our overseas business?' 'Both/and' involves asking questions such as 'How does what we are doing in our overseas business refresh our traditional business?'

Similarly, where leadership time is dedicated to visionary thinking about the future of the business, paradoxical leadership requires these visions to immediately inform today's business. From the opposite perspective, what the business is doing today has to be consistent with current, near future and mid-future requirements.

Paradoxical leadership can be helpful in creating new perspectives to address the challenges of a VUCA world. Specifically, working with the subtleties of paradoxical requirements can provide frameworks for responding to ambiguity that go beyond a simple choice. A paradoxical leadership mindset will treat uncertainty as an opportunity for enhancement, rather than an either/or decision.

16 S McChrystal, *Team of Teams: New Rules of Engagement in a Complex World*, Penguin, 2015, p3.

EXERCISE

Table 2 shows different leadership challenges. Make your selection and consider how you can achieve both/and, rather than either/or. For example, what does it mean for your leadership approach to be both 'responsible' and 'daring'?

Table 2: Paradoxical leadership challenges

Responsibly daring	Confidently humble	Planned flexibility
Close, distant relationships	Listen loudly	Logical intuition
Creative determination	Authentic experimentation	Take charge and let go

2.7 Section summary

In this section we have examined four areas of thinking around modern leadership: authentic pragmatism, charismatic connector, team of teams and paradoxical leadership. You may be more attracted to one or two of these, or find elements of each area that you wish to reflect in your leadership approach. The overriding message is that leadership approaches need to be flexible to meet the challenges of each situation, those you are leading and you. In the next section, we look at how you can optimise the benefits of working with your strengths.

3. Building stronger leadership capability

3.1 Introduction

In this section we suggest strategies for understanding how to choose your behaviours effectively and to adapt your leadership approach. We will also look at some quick wins as you adapt your leadership approach and how you can champion others without diluting your leadership authority.

3.2 Identifying and understanding your leadership motivations and strengths

Deepening awareness of your behavioural strengths begins with identifying those strengths. If you have just emerged from a partner admission examination or a leadership development programme, you may be well informed about your strengths. At other career stages, you may need to kick-start your work – for example by selecting your strengths from an inventory, such as the Strengths Finder 2.0: www.gallup.com/cliftonstrengths/en/strengthsfinder.aspx. This has been widely used by Big 4 partners, and lists 34 'themes' covering strengths such as deliberative, connectedness, futuristic and strategic. A small payment allows access to an online questionnaire which in turn generates a detailed report that highlights your top five strengths and how to use them.

There are different ways of looking at strengths reports such as this. The greatest value may well emerge from working with different perspectives drawn from the model. For example:

(a) Future-proofing – self

As a leader, identify the themes and motivations with which you are less comfortable. You may want to ask yourself and others about how others can support the leadership function in these areas. Alternatively, you may look at development training support.

(b) Future-proofing – team

As a leader, expand the exercise to cover your leadership team. Consider gaps that need to be filled to future-proof business leadership. Examples of recent shifts in leadership team composition include increased emphasis on analytical, inclusion and team building capabilities.

(c) Tracking your personal development as a leader

A further use of leadership strengths reports comes in comparing how your strengths change over time.

- What previous strengths have I stopped deploying regularly, and why?

Revisiting the tool annually can demonstrate how you have adapted your leadership approach to meet different circumstances, and what you may need to change for the future. Such changes may be influenced by external developments or the nature of your practice. For example, moving to lead a practice in Paris will need different strengths to those that served you well in the past in the UK.

You may also need to adapt your strengths as your career progresses. For example, the broader portfolio requirements for a senior partner are likely to require greater strength in understanding the big picture and strategy. Deploying your strengths in detail and experimentation may be less relevant in this role.

Psychological changes may underpin strengths as you age, as shown in Table 3.

Table 3: Psychological changes

Career stage	Concern	Behaviour
Initial	Where am I going?	Own original thoughts, experimentation, seeking greater understanding about possible futures
Developing	What do I need to get where I want to go?	Degree of sacrifice for returns in the future, completing training contracts or other study, investing in clearer vision of future self, building foundations for success
Established	What's my reward?	What do I need to do to have the lifestyle I require?
Approaching the end	How will I be remembered?	What is my legacy? Greater focus on wider social acceptance than further career progress

Source: Adapted from Graves (1970)[17]

(d) New applications for your strengths

Reading the detailed report description of a strength may indicate new ways for you to work with your strengths – for example, a report definition of 'creative' might trigger thoughts of how you are also visionary, innovative and resourceful.

17 CW Graves, "Levels of Existence: An open system theory of values", *Journal of Humanistic Psychology*, October 1970, 10(2), 131–155.

EXERCISE

Think about your strengths, motivations, preferred ways of working, etc. Consider how others might understand what you mean. How might you be misinterpreting how others are describing their strengths, etc?

For example, if you say 'I am a strong networker', is that understood as i) you know thousands of people, but not very well, or ii) that you nurture a smaller number of deeper working relationships? Or something else?

3.3 Strengthening your leadership

We start this section with a question that for many leaders has probably become more familiar given the exceptional circumstances of COVID lockdown:

- What have I learned about myself as a leader in the last year?

For many, lockdown has meant fundamental changes in their leadership approach, with rapid adjustment to quicker decision making amidst greater uncertainty. Many who have reflected on their response to these changes have emphasised the benefit of learning so much about themselves and their businesses.

Time will tell whether the tremendous amount that we have learned in challenging times will be matched in less exceptional years. We suggest that in a VUCA world, there will be plenty to learn about ourselves and our strengths if we are prepared to invest time in ourselves and others. Here are some suggestions for how this might happen.

(a) Make time for personal and team reflection

We are capable of thinking in many ways. However, all too easily we can become comfortable with a dominant way of thinking that suits us and adopt it as a default for all our thoughts. It's like having a car and always driving in the same gear, struggling up a hill in sixth.

- To what extent am I not using the potential of my brain?

Alert to the consequences of cognitive overload, and following the cliché of working smarter not harder, we suggest using more of your brain's flexibility as a valuable tool for future-proofing your career.

Evidence of the benefits of using different parts of your brain is seen in the rapid learning that results from stepping back from a task. Waking with a different perspective after a night's sleep happens where we sleep long enough for our brains to process information in different ways to when we are awake. Walking, preferably in nature, has been shown immediately to improve brain function and, over time, to reduce the onset of Alzheimer's.

Our brains use different neural networks. For example, in creating options, we may favour the salience network which inhibits habitual responses, the central executive network which accesses long-term memory, or the default mode network for thinking imaginatively. These networks generate different perspectives, but only if we allow them to. Accessing all three networks takes time, because we are only capable of using one network at a time. A quick decision reduces our options. More options are available if we have space, and preferably silence, to cycle between the different neural networks.

EXERCISE

Once a week, or more frequently if you wish, dedicate 15 minutes to reflection. If possible, do this outside. You can experiment with the environment in which you work; many find lying on grass and staring at the sky works well. Let your mind wander and then wonder about what you now know about your leadership and what you need to adopt to meet future needs. Don't worry if you doze off – your mind may still be making connections.

(b) Adapt to your audience

Your leadership capability will be strengthened by your ability to consciously adapt to the different audiences that you will encounter in increasingly international settings. With the parallel growth of individualism, your leadership will be strengthened by careful consideration not only of your messages, but also the different ways in which they will be received. Global leaders will need to do a lot more than simply amend their text to say 'hello and welcome' in the first language of their audiences.

What audiences look for and how they receive communication differs in different cultures and demographics. Some audiences will be looking at how relatable you are as a leader before they begin to contemplate what you want to tell them. Here you will need to concentrate more on building rapport. Other audiences will see time spent on building initial rapport as interference in the completion of the task. These differences shouldn't mean rewriting your presentation for each new audience. But it may mean starting with different emphases. For example, introducing yourself in a culturally appropriate way at a point on the scale shown below can enhance or ruin the perception of your leadership strength.

"I'm going to get straight to it."	<<------------------>>	"Let me take a few minutes to introduce myself and tell you how wonderful it is to be with you."

Understanding how you might inadvertently cause offence is also important. For example, leaders are often encouraged to smile more, to communicate confidence and openness. However, the first reaction of a Russian to a smile might be stupidity, and that of an Argentinian, distrust. The more you can ask about what works well for your audience the better.

(c) Recognise when others will lead more effectively than you

From time to time an urgent need for leadership in an area of unfamiliarity emerges. For COVID lockdown, this may have been a sudden and urgent need to ramp up the digital marketing strategy. In May 2020, the growth of the Black Lives Matter agenda following the death of George Floyd raised questions about if and how organisations would respond. Rapid decisions were needed, on a matter for which many leaders found themselves ill prepared.

The larger professional and legal services firms that were viewed to have responded well to these sudden changes appear to have done so after leaders consulted with staff or other advisers better placed to contribute to the organisational response. For example, EY stated: "We have started the conversation with our people, and it is increasingly evident that we haven't done enough."[18]

Similar examples of issues where the most relevant perspectives sit outside the knowledge and experience of leadership will emerge in the future. As the number and complexity of these issues increases, leaders will need to be more alert to the consequences of unchecked emotions and the language that they use. It will be necessary to adopt a strategy that acknowledges what has happened and recognises its impact, before detailing immediate actions and future commitments. This requires working with people who better understand the impact of what has happened and have better ideas about how to respond.

Frequently, this work will be characterised by urgency, unfamiliarity and stress. One step that you can take to be better prepared is to understand how you and your advisers can work together most effectively. To find out more, we spoke with Vikki Leach who specialises in helping organisations to frame appropriate responses.

THOUGHT LEADERSHIP

Vikki Leach *has worked with major business leaders to address change, as a consultant and in senior internal positions. She is founder, Inclusion Consulting Ltd, and diversity and inclusion director at Zalando, a major European online fashion retailer. Previously, she was global head of inclusion and diversity at Kantar, a leading data insights and consulting company.*

18 EY (2020), "EY's commitment to anti-racism in the UK", www.ey.com/en_uk/diversity-inclusiveness/commitment-to-anti-racism-in-the-uk.

Vikki Leach (VL): My work involves partnering with leaders to bring about meaningful improvements in relation to diversity, inclusion, equality and belonging.

Steve Couch (SC): What demonstrates leadership commitment to you, your work and the desired change?

VL: Genuine commitment. I need to understand what has triggered the desired change. Too often, I hear leaders discussing change as desirable to tick boxes, retain customers, stay out of court and avoid reputational damage.

It is different when leaders are prepared to empower me, give me resources, get more involved themselves and make sure the change works through measuring the success. The change impact is potentially much greater if a D&I practitioner reports directly to the leadership team, rather than a change management leader in HR. You really know the difference.

SC: What are the professional challenges in working with leaders on change?

VL: To educate leaders about what is needed from them to achieve the desired change and raising their own awareness before we start talking to staff about the narrative. I also need to help them see what I am trying to achieve for them. It's important that they really mean what they say and that we explore and understand their concerns.

SC: And the personal challenges?

VL: Advising in a strategic way and bringing the business along with you requires patience. You have to be very sure they want to hear what you find. There can be a fine line between presenting the issues and sharing what is needed to change behaviours.

SC: Anything else?

VL: It's about leaders respecting and including the people they employ, to make those people feel valued. It comes down to just good leadership.

At the same time, it is really difficult for many leaders. They may not know how to talk about such sensitive and emotive topics that D&I brings; they may be too frightened to talk about it – if they use the wrong language, what happens? – so they're in a really tough situation.
SC: Thank you.

Being able to bring out the best of what Vikki and similar consultants offer to your organisation will be increasingly relevant in a VUCA world.

3.4 Section summary

In this section we have offered a range of suggestions for strengthening your leadership approach. We have emphasised that nothing is prescribed and there are situations for which a suggested approach will be inappropriate. Our strongest encouragement is to think about your leadership approach in each situation.

4. Strategies for working with emerging leadership approaches

In this final section, we suggest two ideas to help you generate insights into how to anticipate changes in your leadership approach that might be needed in the future.

4.1 Megatrends

The context and requirements of future leadership are unknown. However, there is no shortage of material predicting the challenges that businesses will face in the future. These are widely referred to as megatrends. For example, each of the 'Big 4' global consulting firms offers extensive material on megatrends, ranging from 'Climate change'[19]

19 Deloitte (2021), "Beyond the noise – The megatrends of tomorrow's world", www2.deloitte.com/content/dam/Deloitte/nl/Documents/public-sector/deloitte-nl-ps-megatrends-2ndedition.pdf and KPMG (2021), What are the global megatrends?, https://home.kpmg/xx/en/home/insights/2013/10/what-are-the-global-megatrends.html.

and 'Demographics',[20] to 'Shifts in global economic power'[21] and 'Work and life unbounded'.[22]

Identifying trends that you expect to be most relevant to your current business can inform your evolving leadership approach. Trends such as 'New ways of working', 'The rise of the individual'[23] and 'Civil, civic and equality movements'[24] are already having significant influence on what leaders are required to do.

EXERCISE

Using a SWOT (strengths, weaknesses, opportunities and threats) analysis, consider the impact of the following megatrends on your business and what this means for your leadership approach.

Ageing	Hyperconnectivity	(Global) urbanisation
Shifts in global economic power	Gen Z rising	Resource constraints

- Who will staff your business in 5/10/15 years' time?
- Who will be the customers of your business in 5/10/15 years' time?
- Who will your competitors be in 5/10/15 years' time?

4.2 A coaching approach

Each of the leadership approaches we have examined – charismatic connector, authentic pragmatist, team of teams and paradoxical – has long-term antecedents. For example, Lao Tzu, the founder of philosophical

20 KPMG (2021), "What are the global megatrends?", https://home.kpmg/xx/en/home/insights/2013/10/what-are-the-global-megatrends.html.
21 PwC (2021), "Megatrends", www.pwc.co.uk/issues/megatrends.html.
22 EY (2021), "Are you reframing your future or is the future reframing you?", https://assets.ey.com/content/dam/ey-sites/ey-com/en_gl/topics/megatrends/ey-megatrends-2020.pdf.
23 KPMG (2021), "What are the global megatrends?", https://home.kpmg/xx/en/home/insights/2013/10/what-are-the-global-megatrends.html.
24 Project Management Institute (PMI), Civil, Civic and Equality Movements Megatrends, www.pmi.org/learning/thought-leadership/megatrends/civil-civic-equality-movements.

Taoism provided a counter to super-hero leadership at least 1,500 years ago saying:

> *A leader is best when people barely know he exists, when his work is done, his aim fulfilled, they will say: "We did it ourselves."*[25]

You now have more knowledge of leadership approaches which we hope gives you new ideas for responding to a VUCA world. There is further value in comparing aspects of the different models to develop your leadership approach in changing circumstances. This will be relevant as you lead into the future.

Adaptations and new models of leadership approaches are emerging constantly. As an example, futurist Jamais Cascio has suggested that the expression BANI world should supersede VUCA world.[26] (If your interest is piqued, the details of a BANI world with suggested leadership responses are shown in Table 4.)

Table 4: BANI – brittle, anxious, non-linear and incomprehensible

VUCA	BANI	Explanation	Suggested response
Volatile	Brittle	Susceptible to sudden and catastrophic failure	Resilience Spare resource capacity
Uncertain	Anxious	Every choice is potentially disastrous	Empathy mindfulness
Complex	Non-linear	Cause and effect are seemingly disconnected or disproportionate	Context flexibility
Ambiguous	Incomprehensible	Decisions are made without logic, reason or purpose	Transparency intuition

25 Lao Tzu, original source appears unknown.

26 J Cascio, "Facing the Age of Chaos", *Medium*, 29 April 2020, https://medium.com/@cascio/facing-the-age-of-chaos-b00687b1f51d.

If you are time rich, you might want to read the details of emerging ideas to hone your future leadership approach. But if this is not the case, an effective time-poor approach to evolving your leadership approach is to work with coaching questions. For example, you can periodically revisit how you respond to the coaching question:

- In the next twelve months, how will I adapt my leadership approach to meet changing needs?

This could be more powerful in the context of your business than reading up on BANI.

4.3 Section summary

It is clearly impossible to keep track of every new trend and leadership model, let alone evaluate their worth to your practice. Continuing to reflect on the coaching questions in this chapter, mindful of relevant megatrends, offers a time-effective way of future-proofing your leadership approach.

5. Conclusion

In this chapter we have examined how the function of leadership has changed and what could influence what is required of you in the future. We have shared details of contemporary leadership models, techniques to strengthen your leadership approach and coaching questions to stimulate your thinking, now and in the future.

Chapter VIII: Be collaborative

Steve Couch

This chapter examines different aspects of working in teams.* Teams are now widely viewed as the default operational unit of business. Increasing complexity requires more frequent collaboration to fully address client needs.

The growing need for collaboration is demonstrated by the knowledge doubling curve.[1] This suggests that before 1900, human knowledge doubled roughly every century. By the end of World War II, the knowledge doubling rate was estimated as every 25 years. The current overall rate, which varies depending on the field of knowledge, is viewed as every 13 months. IBM have suggested that the potential of machine learning could eventually see the doubling of human knowledge every 12 hours.[2]

In this context, there is plenty for individuals and organisations to address. Future-proofing will involve more attention to refreshing your networks to work with newly relevant knowledge.

* In this chapter you will find frequent coaching questions. These are designed to encourage you to pause, reflect and then ponder what you are learning and the impact this could have on you and your future practice.

1 FR Buckminster Fuller, *Critical Path*, St Martin's Publishing Group, 1981.

2 P Chamberlain, "Knowledge is not everything", *Design for Health*, February 2020, 4(1), pp1–3.

Reading this chapter will give you more ways to answer the questions:

- How can I build greater trust and collaborate more effectively with others?
- What behaviours are most useful for me when I am working in teams?
- How can my teams maximise our collective potential for greater success?

1. Definitions

1.1 What is collaboration?

Collaboration is a process of working together where, in addition to meeting an agreed objective, each team member is conscious of, and inquisitive about, *how* individual team members and the team collectively work together. Collaboration goes further than each team member performing his/her role. There is also an expectation that each team member will appreciate what is involved in the contribution of each team member, and how this is best incorporated into the whole team.

The notion of the team being greater than the sum of its members and therefore able to offer more, is founded on this appreciation and its potential to deepen collaborative trust. Collaboration can be seen in the openness and curiosity of each team member to experiment based on the collective resources of the team, rather than following individual and/or tried and tested behaviours.

1.2 What is a team?

A team can be distinguished as a group of people who come together for a finite time to achieve shared purposes. It is the focus on shared purposes or team objectives that creates the sense of team as opposed to a group or community where members have different reasons for working together. Teams need a shared understanding of what is offered by, and expected from, individual team members. This understanding will typically develop iteratively over time. Teams will become more aware of individual and combined team member competencies. They will learn from one another to deepen collective understanding of how shared purposes can be achieved.

Later in this chapter we highlight how to be more aware of your team's potential to achieve more and the importance of taking time to do so. Next, we look at the benefits of collaboration.

2. The case for collaboration

In Chapter VII we discussed why individual leaders are having to accept models of collective leadership to meet the challenges of a VUCA world, a world of increasing volatility, uncertainty, complexity and ambiguity.

The case for greater collaboration across organisations emerges from a similar starting point – the requirement to pay more attention to what you are being asked to deliver, rather than starting from what you can offer. Collaboration offers real potential for higher profitability, better opportunities for expanding your organisation's service offering to each client and more appropriate and creative outcomes for clients.

CASE STUDY

A major HR consultancy practice mapped annual fee income from its large client base across six distinct areas of service. The data showed an average service penetration of barely two services per client. The lowest penetration was recorded by the practice's largest service area. There was a positive correlation between higher service penetration and practice profitability. The following year, after targeted work which resulted in service penetration of 2.7 services per client, the practice made significant increases in profitability.

2.1 Higher organisational income and profitability

Collaborative working has been shown to generate new income and increase organisational profitability.

Heidi Gardner's detailed research into US law firms published in her book *Smart Collaboration* (2016)[3] offers a powerful case for collaborative working to increase income and profitability. Gardner addresses barriers to collaboration, including lack of trust in your colleagues, inefficiencies in the collaboration process and your lack of knowledge of your organisation's service offerings. She demonstrates the higher reward available from investing the time needed to overcome such barriers.

- Which practice areas offer the highest potential return for my organisation if we can collaborate more?
- How can I make it more attractive for other practice areas to collaborate with my service area?

In addition to improvements in financial performance, working collaboratively increases the ties between firm and client. This creates higher levels of institutional knowledge for the benefit of both parties. For your firm, benefits include economies of scale that allow more efficient investment in strengthening client relationships. Subject to ethical walls, knowledge sharing is a further benefit. For the client, less time is needed to manage the gaps that can arise when working with different providers.

Given the increasing relevance of this understanding in more complex and uncertain situations, we see greater recognition for partners who grow the amount and range of work that is generated from individual clients. Based on the increased investment needed to pitch for new work, and the greater time needed to learn about a new client, we may see more emphasis on keeping clients and less on winning new clients.

This is not to say that firms should turn exclusively to farming new fees from existing clients. Instead, it is a question of higher relative organisational value from collaborative work to broaden, deepen and better understand clients and their needs.

3 HK Gardner, *Smart Collaboration: How Professionals and Their Firms Succeed by Breaking Down Silos*, Harvard Business Review Press, 2016.

- How might I change the balance between hunting new opportunities and farming existing opportunities to reflect future market changes?

2.2 More appropriate and creative outcomes for clients

Gardner refers to collaboration as the "repeated interactions that, over time, allow the creative combinations of different people's information, perspectives and expertise".[4] In a VUCA world, client demand for original solutions has grown. Increased complexity in business, whether from internationalisation, planned disruptors or the need to address more exceptions, requires more perspectives and diverse thinking. In turn, this means more frequent and wider collaboration. It is important to note Gardner's reference to "repeated interactions" which are necessary for understanding and trust.

Consider also how your business can be more attractive to others looking to collaborate with you, and how you can demonstrate to your clients that you have collaborative skills.

- Which other areas in my network offer the greatest potential for us to create more collaborative offerings for our clients?

In larger firms, this may mean building a business case to employ people with different skills. On a smaller scale the answer may be time for existing team members to develop new capabilities. For example, allowing a hobbyist employee to deepen his/her interest in, say blockchain, may be beneficial for the business and appreciated by the individual.

Where the business case is insufficient to recruit new talent, or develop existing capability, working with external consultants and freelancers may be appropriate. We expect this to become more common.

> EXERCISE
>
> **Identifying opportunities for collaboration**
>
> Opportunities to learn more about your clients go well beyond the boundaries of your firm. In this exercise, we demonstrate a

continued on next page

4 *Ibid.*

collaboration map. The exercise can be used individually or in a team. It can also be used to identify network gaps, which may help to understand how well you are positioned for a future re-tender.

Step 1: At the centre of a flipchart draw two circles, one for your client and one for you or your team or your firm. These are circles in Figure 1.

Step 2: Consider different areas of your network where collaboration may be possible. These are ellipses in Figure 1.

Step 3: Next, be inquisitive about who can help you to make connections in each area. These are rounded corner rectangles in Figure 1.

Step 4: Identify the nature of the connections, to evaluate their strength in supporting collaboration. The rectangles contain some real-life connections.

Step 5: Add empty boxes for Steps 2–4 (see Figure 1). What can you add to these?

2.3 Section summary

We have discussed how building your capability to work collaboratively can enhance your business performance and the relevance of your client service offerings. Our belief is that increasing complexity and

Figure 1: Identifying opportunities for collaboration

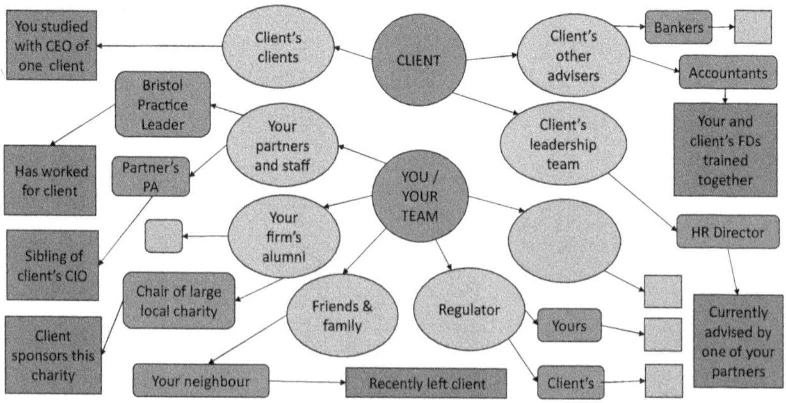

client requirements for tailored advice will see the need for greater collaboration as a given.

3. Understanding how teams work

Compared to the attention we focus on understanding ourselves and others as individuals, we spend little time learning about ourselves in teams. Understanding more about who we are in teams and what influences the way our teams collaborate is becoming increasingly important. In this section we share details about how teams work and suggest steps that you can take to maximise your effectiveness in teams.

- Thinking separately about each team I work in, how do the different behaviours we experience support and hinder team effectiveness?

3.1 How you and your colleagues behave in teams

Early studies to understand how business teams work were conducted by Meredith Belbin in the 1960s.[5] As part of his work on what makes teams more successful, Belbin found that teams where members performed distinct team roles, were more successful than so-called alpha teams made up of the highest performers.

Over time, Belbin identified nine team roles.[6] Although these have been criticised as too prescriptive and unrealistic, there is still value in looking at three areas that the roles cover, namely thinking, action and people. For example, a team lacking thinkers might behave inconsistently and recklessly; a team that ignores people might be selfish and irrelevant; and a team lacking action may not accomplish a great deal.

5 RM Belbin, *Team Roles at Work*, Butterworth Heinemann, 1993.
6 RM Belbin, *Management Teams: Why They Succeed or Fail*, Butterworth Heinemann, 2004.

EXERCISE

Consider a team of which you are a team member. Allocate 100 points across thinking, action and people behaviours that you see. For example, for an action-driven team you might allocate 25 to thinking, 60 to action and 15 to people.

- What does your allocation suggest about potential team strengths and weaknesses?
- Given the team's purpose, what would be the optimum allocation of points for success?
- How can you manage allocations that might otherwise weaken the team's potential?

Contemporary psychometric profiling models, described as 'third generation', have largely moved away from team role identities. Instead emphasis is given to individual and team behaviours based on recent learning from fields including psychology and neuroscience. Models that offer insights on the impact of personal values, different levels of stress and team dynamics offer deeper understanding of individual behavioural preferences and how these can be more effectively utilised in a team.

PSYCHOMETRIC MODELS

PROPHET:[7] Predictive role profiling for high-performing executive teams (PROPHET) offers individual profiles based on motivations, decision-making styles and inclinations. Individual profiles are mapped to a business cycle which runs through create, design, operate and improve. Individual profiles are combined to form a whole team profile that is mapped against the same business cycle to enhance understanding of individual and team potential.

continued on next page

7 PROPHET, www.prophetprofiling.com/.

> **Lumina Spark:**[8] Lumina Spark reveals individual and collective perspectives of values, behaviour, and behaviour under stress, to increase self-awareness and hidden potential. It helps teams to identify potential obstacles in collaboration at individual and team levels.

(a) Building the team

When you are building a new team there is value in investing time on the team's composition. This should involve more than identifying department heads or representatives from the appropriate business areas. Teams need to be formed with individual and collective behaviours in mind. Consider who will offer challenge, energy, calm, independent thought, analysis, reflection and a hard focus on deadlines; consider these in the light of what the team needs to achieve.

For example, the behaviours of a team comprising only department heads, or partners from a single practice area may be too reflective of what is relevant to success in their organisational culture. This may not sit well with what is needed for the most creative thinking that offers more options on the best way to succeed on a specific task.

Team members who know one another well may play expected and familiar roles, further limiting the generation of creative specific solutions. In *Rebel Ideas* (2019), Matthew Syed[9] illustrates the disastrous global consequences of working with team members drawn only from a narrow pool of talents, behaviours and experiences. His chapter headings "Constructive dissent" and "Rebels versus clones" indicate how you might mitigate the impact of a further chapter heading, "Collective blindness".

- How open am I and this team to the creativity that co-opting a 'rebel' could bring to our thinking?

8 Lumina Learning, https://luminalearning.com/.
9 M Syed, *Rebel Ideas: The Power of Diverse Thinking*, John Murray (Publishers), 2019.

- To what extent is my team losing diversity because we have grown too familiar with the same person representing a different perspective?

(b) Maintaining the team

We recommend that you review regularly how effectively the teams in which you work are collaborating. Asking team members for their views on how team performance can be improved and discussing their responses can generate significant improvements in team effectiveness. To gauge the potential benefits, you might want to dedicate the last 10 minutes of each team meeting to asking questions such as:

- What do I see in other teams that might make this team more effective?
- What would allow me to contribute more to this team?

Where important behavioural characteristics are in short supply, consider who else can be brought into the team, or how you and your colleagues can ensure that this behaviour is covered. We have seen that the success of the team may involve you adopting unfamiliar behaviours. For example, this may mean you deliberately stepping away from the detail so that at least one person in the team is looking at the big picture.

- To what extent would the performance of my team improve if I spent time away from my instinctive approach?

CASE STUDY – BONNIE

Bonnie, a UK business unit leader, was assigned to lead her firm's practice in Hong Kong. In UK meetings she had developed a reputation as a quiet listener who offered succinct and influential summaries on what she had heard and what should happen next. In Hong Kong, Bonnie reported that she had found herself sharing much more of what she was thinking at the start of the meeting and asking more open questions to ensure that others shared their views.

3.2 Building team trust

Creating and maintaining trust is vital for teams seeking to achieve more. Higher levels of trust allow increased reliance on colleagues' performance, greater confidence in sharing creative perspectives and the psychological safety to deepen working relationships. This requires spending time together.

The less time invested in building mutual awareness and understanding, the more team members need to rely on inferences and untested assumptions about their colleagues. These increase the likelihood of individual members reaching their own views of what the team should do rather than creating options about what is possible. Further, once these individual views have been established, they can become obstacles to effective team working, if invested with personal ownership and identity.

Higher levels of team collaboration emerge from team members being more open with one another. Deeper awareness of the capabilities of individual team members allows your team to realise more of its potential. It offers the opportunity to generate new team approaches built from creative combinations of team members' capabilities and aspirations.

Our intuitive sense that we build stronger relationships over time is supported by neuroscientific learning. Increasing trust quietens activity in the amygdala, thereby lowering anxiety and stress. Higher trust is also linked to increased levels of oxytocin, associated with good feelings, including empathy and positive thinking. Helpfully, increases in oxytocin levels prompt further trust creating a virtuous circle.

The benefits of oxytocin have been described by researcher Larry Young as "tuning us into social information and allowing us to analyse it at a higher resolution" (cited in Stix, 2014).[10] Greater analytical capability for your teams, is not the only benefit. Trust can be contagious. A team that exhibits trust can make its clients and targets feel more trusting and positive than teams that do not.

10 Gary Stix, "Fact or fiction? Oxytocin is the 'love hormone'", *Scientific American*, 8 September 2014, www.scientificamerican.com/article/fact-or-fiction-oxytocin-is-the-love-hormone/.

EXERCISE

Consider two colleagues: the first, someone with whom you have worked regularly for several years, the second with whom you have a relatively new but established working relationship.

- Identify the elements that contribute to trust and positive feelings in each relationship.
- Which elements from one relationship could you usefully apply to the other?

Different approaches have been developed to accelerate the building of team trust. Contemplation of team-building events can provoke a range of different reactions. For example, some readers will now be recalling with pride or horror the memory of working with strangers to build a bridge over an invisible river using three wooden planks, five lengths of rope and four large beer barrels. Such approaches can work, but the likelihood is that poorly thought through team-building exercises will alienate rather than create greater feelings of inclusion. More straightforward approaches include actively listening to colleagues, sharing hopes and concerns, and respectfully learning more about one another.

EXERCISE

Try this approach for building trust:

- Be at ease – for example, you may want to consciously slow your speaking pace.
- Be curious – ask open questions.
- Actively listen to answers – summarise what you hear.
- Make observations on what you hear.

A significant benefit of this approach is the encouragement that you offer colleagues to share more of themselves with you. This increases trust, collaboration and creative potential.

In his research paper "Breaking Bread: The Functions of Social Eating", published in 2017, anthropologist Robin Dunbar[11] explored the social and individual benefits of eating with others. He found that doing so, particularly at the end of the day, increases trust, engagement and communal relationships. As we spend less time working in shared spaces, it is more likely that we will lose valuable opportunities to learn more about our colleagues. To reduce the impact of this loss, consider the following question:

- How will I ensure the appropriate level of social interaction with colleagues and clients to build and maintain necessary trust?

Potential answers include reviewing how you communicate with others – for example, increased working from home requires you to consider greater use of different types of social communication.

3.3 Building trust internationally

Whether your clients are growing international businesses, or your firm is expanding into new territories, your ability to show sensitivity to cultural difference will be crucial in growing your future business.

- How consciously do I adapt my approach to work with colleagues from different cultural backgrounds?

Small adjustments in your behaviour can demonstrate awareness of cultural difference, which can be powerful in building trust internationally. Avoid stereotypes and demonstrate genuine interest. For example, a little knowledge of significant events in a country's history, its landmarks and geography, and what has contributed to its culture can all demonstrate respect for different cultural values and practices. Even snippets from travel magazines, read at the airport or on the plane, offer information.

Rather than flaunt your knowledge, use what you learn to contribute appropriate responses to what you hear and see, or to inform your

11 RIM Dunbar, "Breaking Bread: The Functions of Social Eating", *Adaptive Human Behavior and Physiology*, 2017, 3(3), pp198–211.

questions. If you are attending a multinational event, one tip is to focus on the nature, history, folklore and cuisine of the venue to share with international colleagues.

For those planning to spend more time working with international teams, models of cultural difference offer insights that can inform how you might build or break trust. Remember that you need to balance potentially valuable insights with stereotypes and assumptions.

HOFSTEDE CULTURAL MODEL

The Hofstede Cultural Model has six behavioural dimensions,[12] one of which is uncertainty avoidance. This is defined as:

The extent to which the members of a culture feel threatened by ambiguous or unknown situations and have created beliefs and institutions that try to avoid these.[13]

The higher the rating, the greater the cultural inclination to control the future.

Selected country ratings:[14]

UK	35	Jamaica	13	China	30	USA	46
Germany	65	France	85	Japan	92	Russia	95

From the ratings, a British person attending an international meeting might want to give more emphasis to planning and briefing, particularly for Russian, Japanese and French delegates. Differences may arise between these country delegates and Chinese delegates who are more comfortable with ambiguity.

12 G Hofstede, (2019), The 6-D model of national culture, https://geerthofstede.com/culture-geert-hofstede-gert-jan-hofstede/6d-model-of-national-culture/.
13 www.hofstede-insights.com/country-comparison/the-usa/.
14 *Ibid.*

Contemporary approaches to developing cultural sensitivity emphasise shared human behaviours rather than individual cultural differences. The behaviours suggested for higher international trust and success include: greater willingness to learn about inter-cultural difference; demonstrating appropriate verbal and non-verbal behaviour when interacting with people from different cultures; aptitude in adapting to new cultural contexts; and curiosity in what causes cultures to develop in different ways. As well as being relevant for international work, these competencies are also relevant for working in multi-cultural domestic environments.

- What competencies do I need to develop in the future to build stronger relationships with those who are culturally different from me?

3.4 Working with team dynamics

The term 'team dynamics' refers to how team members behave collectively and individually. It highlights behaviours that are not brought to the conscious attention and collective discourse of the team. More noticeable examples of team dynamics include the unity of a team paying rapt attention to a speaker, the unobserved frustration of a team member who is being continually interrupted and the lack of collaboration in a team engaged in simultaneous discussions on three different topics.

Greater awareness of team dynamics can remove obstacles and capture more of what the team is doing that contributes to success.

EXERCISE

Sensing team dynamics

This exercise can be particularly useful where your team has lost creativity or direction.

Just before a break, ask your team to look around them and notice where they are and what is around them. Request that they each sit

continued on next page

in a different place and next to different people on their return from a break.

Once reassembled, lead a discussion on the differences team members notice and what this can tell them about how they are working together.

This simple change in interpersonal dynamics can change how the team works.

Trained observers of team dynamics offer a wider awareness of individual and collective feelings in the team. The ability to explore latent behaviours before they otherwise emerge contributes to the team's awareness and trust. Potential problems can be addressed before they build, and more information is available to analyse the team's performance.

- What causes disconnects between what I am saying and what I am feeling in a team environment?
- How aware am I of my behavioural 'leaks' that are inconsistent with the impact I wish to make on others?

EXERCISE

In a team meeting, find the opportunity to dissociate from the team for up to five minutes. Perhaps you can do this during an agenda point where you are unlikely to be involved in the discussion.

Dissociate by imagining yourself looking down on you and the team. Observe what you see from above. Concentrate on the look and feel of the team, the impact of movement and sound on the team, how your colleagues are positioned both in terms of individual posture and in relation to one another. Gradually build a different image of the team. To the extent that it will help the team, share your observations with your colleagues.

3.5 Greater awareness of unconscious influences

Looking back on your behaviour in teams may reveal times when you are proud of your contribution and your team's achievements. Equally, there may be times where you wonder why you behaved in the way that you did. You may still be wondering 'Why did I do that?', or 'What made me say that?' As you increase the range of team members with whom you work, perhaps with more but shorter working relationships, you may benefit from greater awareness of how our subconscious can influence our behaviours.

In this section we offer brief psychodynamic insights that may further your understanding of your behaviours.

Psychodynamics looks at underlying behaviours and feelings, paying attention to what is happening in the unconscious. To demonstrate relevant aspects of psychodynamics, we focus on behaviours in teams.

(a) Projection

Projection takes place when a team member is unconsciously influenced by the emotions of one or more others. It can be beneficial, for example, where the confidence of a single team member increases the confidence of a team. However, projection can also give rise to less helpful behaviours. For example, team members may be unaware that the team has become more argumentative because a colleague had an early morning row with his/her teenage children.

(b) Transference

Transference occurs when a team member (you or a colleague) unconsciously treats another team member in a similar way to how they treated somebody else in the past. Feelings about the past person (who is nowhere to be seen) are transferred to the present colleague. For example, you might treat someone who you don't know well in a similar way to your best school friend because they speak like him/her.

If it were possible to consciously hear the inner dialogue it might be along the lines of 'my colleague reminds me of my best friend when I was sixteen. I will treat him/her as I used to treat my best friend'. This incongruent behaviour is an obstacle to authentic working relations, whether your colleague is consciously aware of it or not.

(c) Countertransference

Countertransference would be seen in the above example if the colleague you were treating like your best friend started subconsciously to behave like your best friend. Influenced by your treatment, your colleague may start treating you in a similar way to how your best friend once treated you.

If both transference and countertransference are present, you are treating your colleague as someone different, and your colleague is treating you from the perspective of someone different.

You can reduce the potential unhelpful influences of projection, transference and countertransference, by questioning why you feel the way you feel about team members, particularly if their behaviour towards you seems variable, perhaps asking:

- Why am I feeling the way I feel about my colleague?

3.6 Section summary

This section has considered ways that you can operate more effectively in teams. We have seen the importance of self-awareness, building team trust and curiosity about individual and team unconsciousness. Working with these areas offers a sound platform for success in the ever-increasing number of teams in which you are likely to be working.

4. Leveraging team resources for efficiency and profitability

In the final section of this chapter we suggest ways that can help and hinder you and your colleagues in your efforts to collaborate as efficiently and profitably as possible. We start with an examination of different resources that may be available to you. We then introduce two models of teamwork and the origins of agile working.

4.1 Resources

(a) You and your colleagues

Arguably the most valuable resources available to your teams are you and your colleagues. Performance is largely dependent on you. No matter whether you are a team sponsor, the person who has commissioned the team to work together to achieve its purpose, the appointed team leader, a senior member of the team or just an ordinary team member, the role you play can be of great significance. This is particularly the case at the outset.

One of the earliest factors that can either make or break team success is commitment of appropriate time to the team's purpose. With the acceleration in knowledge growth and increasing interdependence of multiple workstreams, you may expect less time for you or your team to catch up in meeting its obligations.

- What are the commitments that I have made in the last three months that I will struggle to keep?

You may have anticipated working in a particular team and be ready to do so. However, and more commonly, you may be wondering how to fit a new commitment into an already heavy workload.

Many partners can find it extremely challenging to say 'no' to an opportunity. It may be a fear of missing out, or a sense of not wanting to let others down, that steers you to make further commitments when you already know that you will be busy. Simply agreeing to take on a new challenge can be tempting as it can cause a positive surge of dopamine as your brain reacts to the opportunity for achievement.

The following questions may help you to find the appropriate involvement level of commitment to manage the risks that you will not deliver for the team and that you will become overstressed.

- What else will I be able to achieve by not taking on this commitment?
- How will the increased stress that I will face if I take on this task, impact on this team and its performance?
- Who in my network would benefit if I involved them to reduce my time commitments?

If you cannot reduce your commitment to a particular team, it is appropriate to ask these questions of your work in other teams.

Another factor to consider at the outset and agree, is how the team will work together. Discussions about team working practices, culture and behaviour can play a valuable role in increasing understanding and thereby team trust. This is particularly so when team members have not worked together recently or ever. Further reviews are recommended when existing members leave a team and when new members join. This also applies when there are major changes in how the team operates. For example, where COVID lockdown restrictions change in a country or region, the impact on a team's working practices may be of sufficient significance to merit revised agreements on team working practices.

Functional roles and responsibilities may be over valued in considering who should join a team. Attention to specialist skills, relevant experience, cultural knowledge, and perhaps dedicated training will be as appropriate for teams tasked to meet the challenges of a VUCA world. Time will also be needed to share and understand team member preferences.

CASE STUDY

At the first meeting of a client proposal team, it emerged that all team members shared a strong preference for action-orientated behaviour. This was felt to be at odds with the nature of the client. The team chose to work with a facilitator who would help them to be more considered.

At the instigation of the facilitator, at each meeting team members took turns to silently listen and observe proceedings for 50 minutes. For the last 10 minutes of their allocated hour, the silent team member commented on what they had observed, shared thoughts, summarised and proposed actions.

The team reported that it valued the time engineered for review and reflection. Individual members said that at the end of their hour they had a deeper appreciation of how the team was behaving.

(b) Working with others

The role outlined above can also be played by someone who is independent from the team. This may mean co-opting a colleague or, where appropriate, a small team of colleagues, to observe say half a day's work or a longer Zoom call, before making suggestions for process management (with the option of also commenting on content management, as long as this does not detract from the priority of focusing on process).

There is a range of specialists who the team can work with to achieve higher performance.

(c) Subject matter coach

The choice of a specialist coach will be driven by the team's shared purpose. A team working on a client proposal may choose to work with a proposals coach. Ideally this will be someone who can manage the team process as well as advising the team on the content and appearance of a strong proposal. A presentations coach should offer guidance on the chemistry that the team creates as well as content detail such as the structure of a proposal.

(d) Process facilitator

A process facilitator concentrates on the team process to the extent of not necessarily being aware of what is being said. Facilitation can provide the team with feedback on what has been observed, and suggestions for what to do next. Benefits of facilitation include independence and objectivity. These form the basis of comments weighted more to process and successful completion of the task, rather than to individual issues (ego) which may be acting as obstacles to efficient team operation.

(e) Team coach

Team coaches focus on interactions amongst team members, to create greater awareness of behaviours, including team dynamics, and their impact on the team. Input from the coach is much less directive than from a facilitator based on principles that the team's most effective and sustainable learning is generated from its knowledge of itself. Team coaches will generate opportunities for the team to be more aware of what else might be happening in the team and to agree how best to proceed.

4.2 Working with models of team behaviour

Models of team behaviour have been developed to encourage more effective team working. Here we provide details of two, before briefly examining the Agile Manifesto. Tony Llewellyn's book *The Team Coaching Toolkit*[15] provides more comprehensive coverage with chapters on specific areas such as improving team communication, building team resilience and encouraging learning, innovation and improvement.

(a) Peter Hawkins: The five Cs approach

In *Leadership Team Coaching* (2017), Hawkins has distilled the essential elements of systemic working in teams into five easily remembered disciplines.[16] These are:

Commissioning and recommissioning: Hawkins suggests that to be successful teams need to regularly share and test understanding of the team's purpose and success criteria – a process of initial commissioning and subsequent recommissioning. This includes initial and iterative reviews with the sponsors and stakeholders. Hawkins recognises that understanding of the team's purpose is likely to change and how easily the team may be distracted from its purpose, or for the changing purpose to drift away from the team.

Clarifying: Here, team members learn as a team about their individual and collective understandings of the team's purpose and agree strategies to achieve it. This discipline may involve a discussion of individual and team values.

15 T Llewellyn, *The Team Coaching Toolkit*, Practical Inspiration Publishing, 2017.
16 P Hawkins, *Leadership Team Coaching*, 3rd edition, Kogan Page, 2017.

Co-creating: In this discipline, the team focuses on operational elements of working together. Outputs may include project plans, performance objectives and other measures.

Connecting: This discipline acknowledges that individual teams work within larger systems and need to connect with different parts of the system in appropriate ways. Hawkins suggests four levels of connecting:

- informing (one-way);
- communicating (two-way);
- engagement (eg, with stakeholders who can influence outcomes); and
- partnering (eg, working with other project teams for a time).

Considering that stakeholders frequently complain about not hearing enough from teams, ask yourself:

- How do my teams choose the appropriate level of connecting with each part of the system?

Core learning: This includes reflection on how capacity and potential can be used by individual team members, the team, the wider organisation and beyond. To facilitate core learning, discussions should be scheduled frequently as the team works through its task, rather than just as a post-project review.

(b) Patrick Lencioni: The five dysfunctions of the team

Hawkins' five C's model offers disciplines for more effective process management in a team. In contrast, in *The Five Dysfunctions of a Team* (2002) Patrick Lencioni suggested approaches to increase beneficial team behaviours.[17]

Lencioni's five team dysfunctions and our summaries of how to negate them are shown in Table 1 (overleaf).

17 P Lencioni, *The Five Dysfunctions of a Team*, Jossey-Bass, 2002.

Table 1: Team dysfunctions

Dysfunction	Collaborative team behaviours
Inattention to results	Focus on the achievement of collective results
Avoidance of accountability	Holding one another accountable for delivering plans
Lack of commitment	Commit to decisions and plans of action
Fear of conflict – artificial harmony	Engage in unfiltered conflict around ideas
Absence of trust	Trust one another

Source: Adapted from Lencioni (2002)

Absence of trust: Where team members have not developed trust in each other, individuals spend more time managing their individual behaviours rather than contributing to collective behaviour. Weaknesses and mistakes are defended rather than shared and constructively managed. For Lencioni, the base for team performance is trusting one another.

Fear of conflict: Without trust, team members will find it difficult to engage in what Lencioni calls "productive conflict".[18] Instead, there will be hesitation around how to work with others to maintain "artificial harmony",[19] and/or conflict without concerns for the consequences for the team. Teams that fear conflict are more likely to conduct business in side-meetings and limited distribution emails. Team members who have built trust with one another are well positioned to share conflicting ideas without fear of judgement.

Lack of commitment: Teams will often need to commit to actions before consensus is reached and without complete certainty about the appropriateness of the action. Trust and emphasis on decisions being team decisions and not just individual decisions, should build

18 *Ibid.*
19 *Ibid.*

further to achieve clarity and higher collective commitment to plans of action.

Avoidance of accountability: Here Lencioni refers specifically to the need for team members to challenge substandard performance or behaviours in the team. Accountability is a shared team responsibility.

Inattention to results: Lencioni highlights the possibilities of team members being distracted from meeting the team's shared purposes. Instead, members may be satisfied by what simply being in a team means for them individually or settling scores with each other. Such behaviour needs to be called out and accounted for, to refocus the whole team on its results.

(c) Agile working

The concept of agile working has been a significant addition to the cannon of how teams work together. Agile approaches require teams to actively engage in debate on different perspectives of how to work together. Each team creates and defines its unique approach, rather than following the team leader's familiar and comfortable approach. Agile working originates from software engineers. Their original manifesto states:

AGILE MANIFESTO[20]

We are uncovering better ways of developing software by doing it and helping others do it. Through this work we have come to value:

- *Individuals and interactions over processes and tools.*
- *Working software over comprehensive documentation.*
- *Customer collaboration over contract negotiation.*
- *Responding to change over following a plan.*

While there is value in the items on the right, we value the items on the left more.

© Beck et al, 2001

20 © Agile Alliance. For the full manifesto, visit www.agilealliance.org/agile101/the-agile-manifesto/.

- With reference to the Agile Manifesto, which preferences for better ways of working are appropriate for me and my teams?

4.3 Section summary

Models of team working offer ways of collaborating that are more effective and relevant to the achievement of objectives. They have the potential to enhance how resources, primarily team members, are deployed, for the financial benefit of clients and efficient ways of working. Future ways of working will emerge, many of which will be relevant to the success of your practice.

5. Conclusion

In this chapter, we have looked at the growing relevance of collaboration to your work. We have provided evidence and examples of why collaboration will matter for you and your clients. Our discussions about how you behave in teams, ways of building trust and the role of team dynamics offered awareness and understanding of what may be happening in your teams. We have also suggested ways to operate more effectively in teams and looked at how to use your team resources and models of team working to enhance team processes. We have offered coaching questions to help broaden your current and future thinking.

Chapter IX: Share good ideas

Clare Jones

This chapter explores sharing ideas to achieve higher performance in your legal career. Do you want to be an authority? What is 'thought leadership', and why bother with it? Who is your ideal audience, and what's your strategy for engaging them? How can you build your long-term reputation? How do you measure return on investment and manage risks in becoming known?

1. Why should lawyers share ideas?

Many lawyers are good at writing and talking. They have lots of ideas. They are often hugely creative and are dab hands at coping with immense detail. They use forensic knowledge to help clients every day. Yet, the vast majority of lawyers also keep their brilliance quietly under wraps. Their thoughts, theories and trusted opinions are generally reserved for closed communities.

As a human, lawyer and possibly parent or relative of younger people, you can't fail to have noticed how digital channels have eliminated all barriers of location and resource. Ten years ago, it was rare to see a lawyer comfortably engaging in online conversation. However, that is changing fast. Some, usually more youthful, lawyers blog, write books and post online about diverse topics from fintech to fashion.

Not only can sharing your ideas build your authority, but it can also boost your name recognition, brand power and promote you on social media. It can also make your new prospective client a more informed buyer and augment your sales process. Authorities, experts and industry leaders get most of the sales and profits in any industry. This is why organisations like McKinsey have been publishing their quarterly publication since 1964.

However, despite all the benefits, most lawyers are reluctant to author content. It is a considerable effort, it requires deep pockets, you've got far too much client work to do and you hate 'bigging yourself up'. Yet you are more than capable of communicating engaging, meaningful and relevant ideas; you have highly differentiated skills and knowledge with niche audiences ready to connect and build relationships with 'trusted' advisers. Many businesses act like automatons and are disconnected from their audiences.[1] Much legal content is dull and unimaginative. Why? Is it time to engage and delight a bit more? Thought leadership is an essential tool of differentiation in our disruptive world. If you are not in the conversation, can you be sure your competitor isn't?

Building connections through sharing ideas is a strategic use of a precious resource – your time. If the idea of seeing your name in lights was previously not a goer, let us persuade you to think differently, before you choose to get left behind; perhaps you can even improve your level of visibility in the places that count by incorporating some of these strategies in a low-key way or lessening the burden by collaborating with colleagues.

2. What is a thought leader?

Thought leadership is a relatively new concept, and it means different things to different people. Kate Gibbons, the partner responsible for

1 Julie Lellis and Melissa Eggleston, *The Zombie Business Cure*, New Page Books, 2017.

global knowledge at Clifford Chance, commented in *Legal 500 GC* magazine: "Thought leadership encompasses all opinion-forming interactions, including seminars, round tables and the website. It's about networking, through whichever medium, to share essential insights. It's fun, interesting and intellectually stimulating."[2]

Love it or hate it, the term has caught on and describes a person who is not just a subject-matter expert but also a renowned, go-to authority in their field. Malcolm Gladwell[3] believes that if you practise a skill for enough hours, you'll have a good chance at becoming an expert at it. That's five years of a lawyer's time. You're in the expert club, right?

Author Laurie Young explained that thought leadership offers unique points of view that can be useful and inspiring.[4] Hence, an excellent way to share your value. The vast apparent budgets of the Big 4 and consulting firms salute this concept. In the legal world, thought leadership is less of a phenomenon yet is increasingly used to connect the firm with 'vertical' industry and business trends, build 'star' reputations, showcase technical excellence and do some discreet marketing.

Still not convinced? Sangram Vajre, in an *Inc* article,[5] argues that the term thought leader is egotistical, overused and unrelatable, and in the same unfortunate genre as maven, visionary, guru, rock star, game-changer or entrepreneur, saying, "I once met a guy who called himself a thought leader. That's like saying, 'I have thoughts, and you don't.'" Be called a thought leader by industry and peers, but don't declare yourself a visionary, he warns.

The title of this chapter focuses on sharing *ideas*. TED, the immensely successful global nonpartisan nonprofit, is devoted to spreading such

2 For more, see *Legal 500* article by Kate Gibbons and Lynette Williams, "Thought Leadership: Becoming a leading voice on the issues that matter", www.legal500.com/gc-magazine/feature/thought-leadership-becoming-a-leading-voice-on-the-issues-that-matter/.

3 Malcolm Gladwell, *Outliers: The Story of Success*, Little, Brown and Co, 2008.

4 Laurie Young, *Thought Leadership: Prompting Businesses to Think and Learn*, Kogan Page, 2013.

5 For more see *Inc* article by Sangram Vajre, "3 Reasons You Should Never Call Yourself a Thought Leader", www.inc.com/sangram-vajre/3-reasons-you-should-never-call-yourself-a-thought-leader.html.

ideas, by sharing interesting content and points of view. This is, one could argue, a relatively inoffensive pursuit.

THOUGHT LEADERSHIP

***Chris Rushworth**, director of business development and marketing at TLT LLP, shares his insights on what it means to be a thought leader.*

What is a thought leader?
In describing a thought leader, it's important to separate established expert authorities from lawyers who may wish to comment on a given topic. There is a massive gap. There are very few true 'thought leaders' where you are recognised to be at the cutting edge of your area of expertise, embedded with the key stakeholders (the top firms, industry bodies, regulators, etc), known as an original thinker on a certain issue, region or market and with a strong platform to share your views.

Can anyone become a thought leader?
In theory, it is possible for any lawyer to become the 'go-to person' on a particular topic within their firm and the external market. But, becoming a thought leader takes effort to achieve. You need to build your knowledge, experience and therefore your credibility as well as look at how you creatively share your ideas and insights to build a reputation. It takes planning and focus, but building a stellar reputation in an area that you have a deep interest in has great potential to enhance your career.

How long does it take to become a thought leader?
Thought leadership is a commitment to the long game – but one that pays dividends, with a reputation for true insight difficult to replicate. Disruption and change, particularly in areas like technology and regulation, can create opportunities to carve a niche quickly. But you still need to be relentless in your focus to build genuine expertise and

reputation. You'll know you're making progress when colleagues and clients start to turn to you for insights and advice.

Whilst you may have to push to get the best speaking slots and articles, social media has democratised the opportunity to build your reputation – although it is an increasingly noisy space. No matter the platform, to cut through the same rules apply. Think about your audience; what are they interested in and how can you deliver your ideas in an engaging way that ensures you stand out. This is critical to growing your network and having a platform to share your ideas.

What kind of 'ideas' are best to share?

The best firms focus on a relatively small number of topical issues that will have a significant impact on their clients and help them to grow relationships. They invest heavily in marketing campaigns that position them as experts and create conversations with clients.

As an individual lawyer, you may want to focus on one part of a more extensive firm-wide campaign or find your niche area of expertise. You can choose very topical issues that may be short-lived or use a process of 'horizon scanning' to spot problems that will affect clients in the years ahead. Don't limit yourself to legal and regulatory changes, as market developments may provide better opportunities for thought leadership.

Beware of generic topics that have already been heavily covered, like 'digital transformation' as you'll be competing with a myriad of reports and articles from other thought leaders. Instead, find your angle that will resonate with your clients. And, don't fall into the trap of thinking you need to produce a whole load of original material. You don't, but you need a strong point of view, and you need to be good at communicating it.

The key is not to make assumptions about what clients view as important but to find things they care about. Take every opportunity to speak to your client about the issues affecting them and test your ideas before investing heavily in them.

Which platforms are best to share those ideas?

You need to separate the content [the ideas] from the platform or channel. 'Digital first' is a key trend, and speed is vital. You do not want to be the last person to share the same idea on a niche topic – if you are late to the party, think about what you can add to take the topic forward.

You can share your ideas through a whole host of channels, from your firm's website and social media accounts to established media outlets. Choose formats that work for your clients and targets, be that short articles, videos, podcasts, or downloadable tools and summaries.

You can mix different content styles too – whether that's short-form views like 'five top trends' or 'an intro to…', to longer-form content on platforms like LinkedIn. It doesn't have to be 100-page reports – design what you write and how you deliver it to suit your audience. Being visible on camera is valuable, despite the cringe factor, and brings you to life. You are much more likely to get recognised in future and build your brand.

Who can help with establishing a person as a thought leader?

Your marketing department, if you have one, is your great ally. Otherwise, you should look to hire a marketing professional. They will not generate the insights for you but they will be your critical friend, helping you clarify who your content is for and what the value is to that audience. Then, they will be able to work with you to bring your ideas to life in an appropriate and engaging format. They can also play an important role in giving you confidence during the process of 'putting yourself out there', with the added comfort that you've verified that an audience exists for your topic.

Are there any risks involved in building a reputation?

You may want to steer clear of controversial topics – but speak to your wider team and your firm's press team about this. There may be angles or ways to engage that you hadn't thought about. There might also be issues to consider around how particular comments or ideas land with your firm's wider client base. Being public about your views and opinions is not without risk and requires careful consideration, but you can navigate these challenges and draw on the experts in your business to help mitigate any risks.

How can someone know that their thought leadership efforts are working?

Marketing is hugely measurable. You can set several key performance indicators to measure the performance of your efforts both internally and externally. You can track reputation and brand value, including tactical elements such as clicks, likes, comments on social media, press mentions, conference invitations, etc.

Ultimately, thought leadership success depends on how you use it to support clients, build relationships and eventually, how it helps you win work. Therefore, you should regularly ask yourself, 'how much am I consulted internally?', 'how many clients have I talked to about this?', 'how many pitches has this led to?', 'how is my view on the topic evolving?'. This is a virtuous circle, where the conversations you're having enhance both your ideas and your marketing efforts simultaneously. It takes time, but an investment in thought leadership can create immense long-term value for you and your firm.

3. Who is in your tribe?

Since building a relationship with your desired audience is your end goal, let's get to know them better. "Tribes", as coined by Seth Godin[6] in his 2008 book, are your people. They are everywhere, and they're waiting to connect to leaders with shared values. Tribes are earned, not spammed, and once they engage with you, they become your promoters,

6 Seth Godin, *Tribes: We Need You to Lead Us*, Portfolio Penguin, 2008.

advocates and referrers for life. Who matters to you? Who needs to see your ideas? Who is in your tribe?

Audience personas are the secret weapon to knowing your tribe. These are fictional representations of your typical audience. You'll go back to them repeatedly and find them invaluable in everything you write (that is not legal!) to clients and contacts going forward. Let's step into the shoes of these people and understand how they perceive the world.

Start by listing 3–5 types of people ('personas') that tend to be your typical clients, aspirational clients and any other kinds of people you'd like to influence (eg, regulator or media). You might decide these personas have different roles – eg, general counsel, HR director, CEOs, accountancy partner, law firm partner, journalist.

Ask yourself some coaching questions:

- Do you have any critical/distinctive demographics that need to hear from you?
- What are these people good at?
- Can you comment on their motivations?
- What are their habits and preferences?
- What is not essential to them?
- What newspapers do they read?
- What are their political tendencies?
- Where do these people spend their time, both virtually and in person?
- What might concern them at the moment?
- What might excite them at the moment?

Are there any common themes or areas you feel similar to? Are there patterns, themes or clues as to how you might craft your approach to content?

You can now create personas, just as brands do: detailing the characteristics of the most stereotypical types of people you seek to engage with. Make them pointed and exaggerated, and you can even give them names and add illustrations or images. You may even produce a work of art you can stick on your office wall.

Refer to your personas when producing content, even when you write an email, to ensure you get the tone and content spot on. Without personas, you quickly revert to type, communicating for your needs, not theirs. This won't gain traction with today's audience.

4. Who is your competition?

Globally, the legal market is vast and increasingly fragmented. There are around 150,000 solicitors holding practising certificates in England and Wales and over 1.3 million attorneys in the US. You've got competition, but don't despair. There is no one like you. You can also learn from your rivals. Research the leading legal voices in your practice area. Jot down some thoughts on your impression of their approach. Perhaps, it's time to 'model' their excellence or learn from their errors?

Some coaching questions you can ask are:

- What content do they produce?
- What platforms are they on (LinkedIn, website, articles, etc)?
- What was your intuitive overall impression?
- What are their strategies, strengths and weaknesses?
- What does this say about their expertise?
- How would you describe the visual impact of their content and personal style?
- What is the tone of voice of their writing?
- What resources, effort and frame of mind might they have had?
- What ideas can you take away?

5. What type of content will you share?

Content is the vehicle by which you'll share your ideas, and it is happening across all industries, including professional services. It comes in a dizzying array of formats, including blogs, case studies, reports, e-books, infographics, images, checklists, podcasts, videos, books, seminars, roundtables, slide decks, social media posts, and the list goes on. We communicate in so many ways every day, both verbally (written, orally and visually) and non-verbally; the possibilities for expressing your content are virtually unlimited. Which format are you drawn to most? Which repels you?

So what type of content is right for you? The first consideration is your appetite. Many of you will simply not have the resources for a high degree of effort, exposure or risk. If you have a marketing department or PR agency, they will be able to help. Otherwise, you will need to consider ROI and tread carefully. High effort content usually involves lots of research and writing such as books, reports, white papers, presentations and blog posts. Your content will be more conversational at the medium effort level, such as videos, podcast appearances and contributing to social media debates. Your name will appear on other people's content at the lowest effort level, or you'll be seen in testimonials. You will also prefer certain media over others. There is no value in deciding that you need to start vlogging if you can't stand seeing yourself on camera.

Some coaching questions you can ask yourself about your content choices are:

- What level of appetite do you have for producing 'content' from your ideas?
- How is your voice different from your competitors? How might you make it stand out more?
- Who is your audience, and what do they want to hear, see or experience?
- Which are the best channels for you to raise your profile (for example, blogs, case studies, reports, articles, books, speaking, podcasting, social media, webinars, infographics, etc)?
- What help can you get to produce and hone your content?
- What are the first steps you need to take to bring your ideas to your audience?

THOUGHT LEADERSHIP

Prolific ideas sharer ***Rosie Burbidge****, intellectual property lawyer and partner at gunnercooke LLP, gives an insight into content strategy.*

Rosie explains that her objectives with her content strategy are to showcase her knowledge of IP, fashion and gaming, and retail and technology in the broader sense. She also aims to demonstrate that she is approachable, embraces technology (including legal technology), and shares her sense of humour and personality.

Rosie produces content in various formats, including websites and blogs, and has a strong presence across three social media channels. She has also recently published a book, *European Fashion Law: A Practical Guide from Start-up to Global Success*, which has been a considerable effort, but worthwhile in confirming her authority in one of her key markets.

Some groundwork has gone into building Rosie's reputation. She used to be a blogger for IPKat, an iconic platform in the IP community and has clocked up tens of millions of page views. This, she feels, has had substantial value in building her reputation. She also acknowledges the importance of her early career in super relevant, high-calibre IP firms such as Olswang, which adds "cachet".

Her clients use and engage in a range of content channels. For example, Instagram is a key channel for the fashion industry. Whilst Rosie maintains a presence on the platform; this is not where her fashion clients would expect their lawyer to engage. Her in-house clients are more likely to engage with her on LinkedIn, but she accepts her efforts are "not frequent and selective". Rosie acknowledges there is scope to engage more but is also wary of overkill. She says, "people only want short insights into things they need to be thinking about". One format that can work well is to provide 'what you need to know' information and 'checklists'.

In terms of brand voice, Rosie is clear: "I think it is important to be straightforward, succinct, practical, and to use engaging, accessible language." For example, she would use "dispute" rather than "litigation". Ultimately, Rosie says: "You need to be a bit more *Guardian* than legalistic. It goes wrong when someone tries to talk about something they don't know about, such as abstract areas of law or business. If you write about something, you deal with regularly it is much easier to engage with the audience."

Interestingly, as a lawyer in a 'challenger firm' and essentially her own boss, Rosie appreciates her intellectual freedom compared with competitors: "The big advantage I have is that I don't have to get content cleared before posting. I decide what I publish, whereas they might write a more technical and detailed article, then the approval process may make it even less appealing."

Rosie runs a bustling practice and producing content is a challenge. She is experimenting with writing support. However, she cautions, "I don't think you can give too much of that away. Imagine someone quizzes you on an article you've written, and you have not done the groundwork."

For the reluctant ideas sharer, Rosie advises proactivity and to find pleasure in the process. In her experience, "worrying about what to post took longer than posting. The thing I realised is that actually very few people read it even if they like it or share it." She continues, "I enjoy sharing content – it's an opportunity to help others and engage with more people."

For Rosie, the return on investment is difficult to measure. "It's marketing, and the end game is to be in the running. And not be discredited because you are not in a big-name firm or at the top of directories. How do you measure the success of advertising? Even if you measure clicks or purchases, that doesn't tell the full story. It isn't easy to measure success because it is abstract." Rosie has discovered that she has been included in the list of people to contact in quite big companies. "That's because someone has seen something I've written and recommended my services. That is the product of thought leadership. It's a no brainer. You should do it."

6. What's your content strategy?

The idea is to write so that people can hear it and it slides through the brain and goes straight to the heart.
Maya Angelou[7]

6.1 Get the basics right

(a) What have you done so far?

The first thing you need to do is reflect on and refresh your content efforts. That includes any content on your website (including your biography), your LinkedIn profile or Twitter bio. Most people need to do a better job on LinkedIn. Using it to its total capacity is a whole topic in itself. However, in the meantime, you can make a great start by viewing your profile from a 'tribe' perspective, using all the fantastic LinkedIn training available for free on the platform and writing a 'tribe-friendly' profile and headline that reflect all your new insights.

(b) Why you?

Why are you writing about this topic, and what makes you the go-to person to comment on it? If you are not feeling the buzz about your subject, who else will it excite? Your readers will be asking themselves these questions.

(c) Why now?

Timing is everything, and there is a range of possible prompts behind your choice of topic. Maybe the time of year is relevant, or you're

7 www.goodreads.com/quotes/153402-the-idea-is-to-write-it-so-that-people-hear.

writing about something in the news? Are you coming in early on this issue, or might your perspective get lost? It's OK to create content on a popular subject; you just need to find an interesting angle that no one else has.

6.2 Clarify your tone of voice

Establishing the right tone of voice is something large brands spend a fortune on. The idea is that every communication is consistent and feels familiar, so the audience builds trust and knows what to expect. Think about your favourite brands. They all have a unique way of speaking to you and sharing their personality. What's yours?

You always have the same voice in real life, but you'll use a different tone depending on the situation. Once you've considered the needs of your audience personas, what dimensions of your tone of voice are essential? For example, how formal or friendly does your content need to be? Do you need to be conversational, educational, informative or humorous? How can you articulate this in your communication? For instance, 'when I write, I like to be brief, positive and direct'. Of course, you can make adjustments, but it is time to 'own it'. You're selling yourself, your image and your reputation. What you say should be appropriate for you. You should be able to communicate effortlessly in any circumstance, whether it's a one-minute introduction to an online seminar, a pitch to an important prospect or a white paper.

6.3 Power up your brand

'Personal branding' refers to the practice of presenting yourself, your career and the experience as if you are a brand. Whether you like it or not, you always project an image, impression and identity. Does that promote trust, authority and influence? Digital marketing, and mainly social media, has made personal branding more popular and increasingly important. Content marketing is the perfect method to grow your brand, but remember, the goal is not to sell. See yourself as a journalist sharing information, a perspective and ideas, not selling services.

6.4 Tell stories

Stories and storytelling are in vogue at the moment. However, such accounts have been around for thousands of years. From Stanford to Wharton, leading business schools teach storytelling as a hallmark of effective leadership and executive presence. A good story is scientifically proven to be more effective in helping people remember critical information. According to marketing professor Jennifer Aaker at Stanford's Graduate School of Business, stories are remembered 22 times more than facts.[8]

Guy Kawasaki, in his seminal marketing book *Enchantment* (2011), advocates the power of the personal story in engaging others. However, he cautions that to stop them in their tracks one's offering must be quite incredible.[9] No small order, but how can you get some of this across in your messaging? If you are producing 'thought leadership' content from scratch, you'll need to get beyond data and think about how you may be able to craft a story. Here are some coaching questions to get you started on your storytelling journey:

- How can you best communicate your story in a compelling, relatable and authentic way?
- How well do your online bios reflect your story?
- Who are your clients? Whose names can you drop?
- Are there case studies/quotes you can use when illustrating a point? Which clients are willing to tell their story?
- Which facts and figures prove your message? Which examples can you share?
- What is the human side of the topic you're working on?
- What is your personal experience of this?

8 Jennifer Aaker, "Harnessing the Power of Stories", Stanford University VMware Women's Leadership Innovation Lab, https://womensleadership.stanford.edu/stories#:~:text=%22Stories%20are%20remembered%20up%20to,times%20more%20than%20facts%20alone.%22&text=In%20this%20way%2C%20story%20is,as%20a%20tool%20to%20persuade.

9 Guy Kawasaki, *Enchantment*, Portfolio Penguin, 2011.

- What's new in your clients' industries/law? What will your sector/area look like next year, in five or ten years?
- What are your clients' questions, worries, pain points, challenges, and what keeps them up at night?
- How can you make your prospective client a better and wiser buyer?

Andy Weir, author of *The Martian* (2011) recommends that you uncover what is different and special to engage people. This might take some time and you should not be concerned about the precise communication you will want to share; rather get to the meaty bit first, then do your work on crafting your message.[10]

7. How do you make it happen in practice?

Let's face it – you're a busy lawyer. The bottom line is to be clear about goals, honest about the time and effort you're willing to put in and the channels you prefer, and decide on some measures of success.

Like any good plan, you need to know what resources you'll need, when you will begin to deliver value, and how it will all be accomplished. For this to work, it will need to meet the preferences of your audience personas and you. It might help to ask some questions:

- For what do you want to be known?
- Who do you need to influence, and how will you know you've done so?
- What are the right platforms or channels?
- What's your favourite way to communicate?
- What is the best format for your content?
- What simple set of routines will work for you (eg, working on one channel at a time)?
- What will be your success metrics?

Sam Makad, writing on the blog TNS (2020),[11] has practical suggestions for lawyers: "Write articles based on legal insights, share something

10 Interview with Clare McDermott of the Content Marketing Association (CMA) in 2017, https://contentmarketinginstitute.com/2017/03/andy-weir-storytelling-process/.

11 TNS (2020), https://thenextscoop.com/content-ideas-for-lawyers/.

humorous, update on the news about the firm, share quotes, comment on news stories, share behind the scene photos or videos, ask questions and make recommendations."

Create yourself a schedule and get time in your diary. How much time can you realistically spare? Would 15 minutes a day on LinkedIn be of benefit? Many software tools can help you with many of their essential features for free. You can dictate your thoughts and have them turned into writing with Otter AI; improve your writing with Grammarly; manage your 'inbound pipeline' with Hubspot; and schedule email and social media content with Mailchimp, Hootsuite or Buffer. New low-cost AI-based software is emerging all of the time. There are also resources and tools that you may be able to access through your organisation. Hopefully, you'll have a brilliant marketing and business development team who will have ideas to add to your thoughts. Many law firms even provide writers. Don't be afraid to marshal all the help you can get.

You can also think about trying a 'campaign' initiative. For example, you might decide your target is to build a new specialism in your practice. You will arrange one webinar a quarter and a daily 10 minutes on LinkedIn at 10am to comment on and share other people's posts (and promote the webinar). You'll also market the webinar by email. You'll measure engagement, attendees and results. Baby steps.

8. How can you measure the success of your content efforts?

Your goal as legal content creators is to build an audience that can become clients over time. It's feasible to set all manner of metrics with digital channels, but you have to trust that marketing, ultimately, pays off at the end of the day. That might happen in strange and beautiful ways.

9. How do you share good ideas in the long term?

First of all, you need to be honest. How visible are you and how much exposure do you need or want in your career? Is it essential that you develop a reputation as a leader in your field? It's critical to be honest with yourself. Which of the following three scenarios best describe your mindset at the moment?

1. *No exposure, thank you.* If you're not convinced that the world needs your good ideas and that you can get plenty of clients and keep competitors at bay by ignoring the online conversation and going about your business just as you do, that's your choice.
2. *On the fence.* In this situation, we believe there is an option for you to 'share good ideas lightly'. You can work out who your audience is, what they need and zero in on just one channel they are on. First of all, check your online presence is authentic, compelling and congruent (for your audience). Then start to build connections and set yourself a schedule to check in, like and comment on their posts. Be as generous and insightful as you are in real life. It will elevate your online presence, and it may even give you the taste to do more.
3. *Ready to record.* That's great. We have recommended a range of approaches you can use above. However, you also need to manage risk. In 2018, Forbes Coaches Council members commented on their website on the most significant mistakes leaders make with thought leadership. They pointed out that many individuals have too broad a focus and have hastily published poor (often ghost-written), theory-heavy content.[12] You'll miss the opportunity of sharing your point of view and unique stories. It's not wise to be too sales-y or aggressive. Sharing ideas is about knowledge, research and problem-solving. It's about delivering the value and must answer the question, 'What do people need, and how am I providing that to them?'

12 Forbes Coaches Council, "13 Thought Leadership Mistakes That Can Tarnish Your Personal Brand", *Forbes*, 8 March 2018, www.forbes.com/sites/forbescoachescouncil/2018/03/08/13-thought-leadership-mistakes-that-can-tarnish-your-personal-brand/?sh=775c78302b03.

10. Conclusion

Now it's time to be accountable to the good ideas guru in your midst: you!

What are the key action points from reading this chapter? Here are 10 final coaching questions to ask yourself right now. Feel free to add more.

1. What is my understanding of thought leadership?
2. Do I want to be a thought leader?
3. Who is my ideal audience for my ideas?
4. What does my audience want most from me?
5. How can I best articulate my unique point of view?
6. Which are my best channels (for example, blogs, case studies, reports, articles, books, speaking, podcasting, social media, webinars, infographics, etc)?
7. What are the first steps I need to take to bring my ideas to my audience?
8. How will I measure the benefit of my efforts to build my reputation?
9. How will I protect my reputation and manage any reputational risks?
10. What help can I get to produce and hone my content?

Those of you not convinced you have the time, inclination or skills to become a legal content marketer, do not despair. There is always room to be quietly helpful and supportive. You can help colleagues, write segments of content for their publications, step onto their webinar or Facebook Live appearances to support them, and find other small ways to contribute. You can always like and comment on other people's posts on LinkedIn (a highly effective strategy to win friends and influence people) and forward applicable 'saw this and thought of you' posts on your feeds.

Don't you know what we are talking about? Fair enough. You have to be true to yourself, but please don't put your head in the sand. Content marketing is here to stay, and you now know what is involved and may find your unique way to dip your toe in the water.

Whatever your area of legal expertise and whoever you are, you own your reputation. If you don't take responsibility for developing it, others in your space will take bandwidth and corner all of the attention. Sharing good ideas is a core area of your professional development and number nine of the essential career-building tools that will build you a life-long buffer for quieter times and help get you the next job. Good luck. Enjoy being an excellent communicator, sharing brilliant ideas. May your authority glow!

Chapter X: Manage change

Clare Jones

The omnipotent topic of change appears to be a core constant in our disruptive world. Whatever stage you entered law or are in your career now, change most certainly impacts you. Let's explore what change is, how it affects you, how to cope and thrive in changing times and what changes are coming your way.

> *The best way to predict your future is to create it.*
> Abraham Lincoln[1]

1. What is 'change'?

Change is defined as "to make or become different" by the Cambridge Dictionary.[2] Nothing stays the same, and our choices around change are only limited to ourselves. We were all reminded of this fact of life in 2020.

Transition and transformation are certainly endemic in the world of business (and beyond), and the pressure for them comes from many different directions. You certainly don't need a crystal ball to predict the

1 www.goodreads.com/quotes/328848-the-best-way-to-predict-your-future-is-to-create.
2 https://dictionary.cambridge.org/dictionary/english/change.

continuing acceleration of sweeping, breath-taking change across every business sector. In particular, technology has impacted every model, process and interaction over the past few decades. Our prevailing systems continue to reshape and surprise while society evolves to become more complex and specialised.

Over the past few decades, 'change management' has emerged and developed from basic understanding to a core management discipline. The 'chief transformation officer' has arrived in the boardroom with the remit of ambitiously driving forward growth targets.

Anticipating the future is an essential element of future-proofing your career. Indeed, there is no shortage of insights into our future world. Every consultancy and professional service firm worth its salt continues to publish glossy reports purporting its supremacy as an authority on 'megatrends'. Dissecting every social, legal, economic, political and technological aspect of change and its meaning appears to be a thriving industry. We are bombarded with, sometimes dystopic, predictions, particularly on AI, machine learning and robots. We could also be easily seduced and excited by the vast opportunities mentioned.

Some of the many themes discussed will be relevant to you and your life, and many will not. We invite you to type 'megatrend' into a search engine for the latest insights. Pick three authorities you respect and have a quick look through what they have to say. Ask yourself these questions:

- When I read about megatrends, how do I feel?
- What do I feel most excited (or daunted) by?
- Which trend(s) most impact(s) my areas of practice and relevant business sectors?
- What do I offer in terms of skills relating to these megatrends?
- What might I need to work on to realise these megatrends?
- What do these megatrends mean for my future career (opportunities and threats)?

2. What is your relationship with change?

The world as we have created it is a process of our thinking. It cannot be changed without changing our thinking.
Albert Einstein[3]

How you tend to interface with change is likely to be the primary predictor of its impact on you. Levels of comfort around change vary, and many of us can struggle with it. Clinging on to familiar models and approaches is a tempting strategy, whilst change may mean letting go of things reluctantly or starting new, perhaps different, things. Unfamiliar territory may take you somewhere entirely new. Even if you welcome this (eventually), you may experience a rollercoaster of emotions. Change can be brilliant, exhilarating and joyful. Turning over a new leaf can be the best thing that ever happened to you; it can also be very difficult for humans.

Change will not come if we wait for some other person or if we wait for some other time. We are the ones we've been waiting for. We are the change that we seek.
Barack Obama[4]

Your stance on change is likely to depend on the type of change and your role. Not all changes have quite the same meaning or impact. Some are radical and headline-making but others are less important or seem less exciting on paper, yet fundamental effects. For example, minor changes in day-to-day systems, methods or procedures, in the location of an office or desk, in team structures or job titles can add to high impact and cause great sensitivity for individuals. Mergers or large-scale technology changes and layoffs make the headlines more quickly. The other important consideration is if the change is being imposed on you or is planned. Are you a victim

3 www.goodreads.com/quotes/1799-the-world-as-we-have-created-it-is-a-process.
4 www.nytimes.com/2008/02/05/us/politics/05text-obama.html.

or taking responsibility? Have you been consulted, involved or even the change initiator?

Tumultuous, challenging times or an opportunity like never before? Your experience (right back to your early childhood) and filters will undoubtedly inform your stance. For many, change gives rise to intense emotions and fears. They feel victimised and change seems to be something that happens to them; they have no control over it and it can be overwhelming. It's a natural human reaction to resist change.

However, it is also interesting to meet people who give the appearance of breezing through immense external change, even designing it themselves. Those change-makers can plant and develop the seeds of change; they are creators, innovators, people-mobilisers and go-getters. They are eternal optimists who have their eye on the future. While such change leaders have traditionally been marginal outsiders, mad scientists and activists (think Elon Musk), change leadership is fast becoming a virtual boardroom and career-enhancing skill.

2.1 What is your change personality?

You'll cope with change according to everything mentioned above. What type of change personality do you have? Skim through the following questions to provoke your honest thinking. You might like to enlist some help from someone you trust and will be prepared to be honest!

- Where do you fit on the scale between being a resisting reactionary to a curious, communicative change-lover?
- Is change a problem to be solved and overcome, or is it a headache?
- Are you rooted in the past or excited by the future and inspired to share how it might look?
- Are you ready to think and talk about what and why change is valuable?
- Have you thought about the change(s) that may impact others involved and how best to position it as beneficial to them?
- Do you know how to make the change happen yourself?

- Are you ready to provide support to others, including leaders, to manage transition and transformation?
- Are you fundamentally an optimist, or are you more likely to be the 'glass half empty' person?

2.2 What is your concept of change?

Everyone has a unique take on change. Ask yourself:

- What have been the most significant changes you've seen in your life and career so far?
- How have these changes impacted you?
- How turbulent has your life and career been so far?
- Do you think you have experienced more than average change? Why (or why not)?
- Have *you* changed much as a result?
- People say life is short. What is your take?
- How long is your 'now'?
- How 'present' do you think you are?
- If you didn't know you, how old do you think you would put yourself at?
- Imagine yourself in the future – what might you want to tell yourself now about the changes ahead?

2.3 What is your level of resistance to change?

The manifestation of human opposition to change can take many forms. Some people will become quiet or temporarily disillusioned and output may drop off, whilst others will argue, sulk, become wildcats or quit!

Does change make you feel:

- Uncomfortable, awkward or emotional?
- Concerned about what you might lose?
- Is it isolated and disconnected?
- Are you overwhelmed and lacking in energy or focus?

- Simply not ready and dreading each day?
- You are worried about how you can do your job with fewer resources?
- Reflective and nostalgic about the past?
- Angry, bewildered and unable to cope?

These are all common reactions, and it is essential to be aware of your feelings and those around you about change. If you're feeling affected by change that has arrived in your workplace, you can be sure you are not alone. Reaching out to others to receive and offer support is critical, and some organisations are better at institutionalising this than others. What's stopping you from taking the initiative and creating an open dialogue? Remember that gearing up for change can be terrifying, but staying put or shutting down can be just as scary (or even more damaging).

3. What changes are coming for the legal sector?

And as we've explored in previous chapters, the future of legal is a hot topic. The legal landscape is changing as dramatically as any other business sector.

Wouldn't it be nice to find a list, a solution or a crystal ball to provide you with everything you might need to know to leverage change and protect and enhance your future legal career? Having a 'growth mindset', where you are open to upskilling yourself, might be advisable. Also, it will be essential to keep listening to clients to understand and perhaps anticipate their changing needs.

THOUGHT LEADERSHIP

Below are some thoughts from ***Chris Georgiou****, partner and head of Ashurst ADVANCE, on what Ashurst lawyers are doing to manage change and what you might need to think about.*

The biggest theme running through the legal profession today is change, and more than that, truly transformative change. That is something we have not seen before in our professional lifetimes, at least not at this accelerated pace. As a profession, we are starting to embrace that, but it does not come naturally. Today's lawyers need to become not just comfortable with change, but to own and drive it. This is essential if we want to remain relevant to our clients, competitive against market disruption and fit for an increasingly digital future.

But what does transformation mean for the legal profession and for individual lawyers? It means new ways of thinking, new ways of delivering our services, delivering new services, developing new skills and bringing in new types of professionals alongside lawyers. Law in the future does not just mean lawyers, and increasingly does not just mean law... In fact, the business has never involved just lawyers as our services could not be delivered without an army of high-quality professionals supporting the lawyers. The difference now is that many of those 'non-legal' professionals are now front-line, not just supporting lawyers but a core part of the service that is being delivered to our clients, and providing the unique value which complements the legal expertise.

Let's start with thinking (always a good place to start!). The concept of 'design thinking' would have sounded alien to many lawyers even a few years ago, something more appropriate for the 'creative professions', a bit 'artsy'. Now we are upskilling many of our lawyers in this technique, and I would encourage everyone to try it. Ultimately, it provides a fresh approach to problem-solving and creating solutions to our clients' business challenges. We know that one of the most attractive facets of the legal profession to new members is problem-solving, and this is the kind of skill that will excite and motivate younger lawyers and contribute to their development.

New ways of delivering services include the deployment of process engineering, project management, technology and cost-efficient resourcing to promote greater efficiency and save our clients money. But it is not all about reducing cost. Newer operating models such as these offer additional value, such as helping our clients increase speed to market of their own products and services, improving their own customers' lifecycle journey, reducing risk and increasing confidence in the delivery of large-scale projects.

There is also a drive to use technology to make the expertise that we provide to our clients more useful. It is no longer sufficient to present expertise in a static and dry way that lives in a document, unseen and unloved, sitting in the email inbox of the recipient. That expertise needs to be accessible and usable in different ways by all relevant stakeholders within the client. Packaging expertise in a customisable digital format is a powerful way to achieve that.

At Ashurst, we are driving the process of change in many ways, including through our Ashurst Advance NewLaw division. We are conducting our own legal transformation programme within the firm, as well as helping our clients with their own transformation journeys, sharing insights and best practice and building networks of like-minded legal operations professionals. The firm has also recently launched its Ashurst Consulting business, a very significant business that is 'adjacent' to the practice of law, and further evidence of the firm's commitment to push the boundaries and make us future fit.

This is an exciting time once again to forge a career in the profession. It feels like a voyage into the unknown as we reimagine what it means to be a lawyer and a legal services professional!

4. How is change impacting your organisation?

You're reading this book to develop your career. Depending on your position – lone wolf or corporate cog – in an interconnected business environment, it may be helpful to consider a change from a broader, more holistic organisational perspective.

People and processes are often complicated, intertwined and institutionalised. Indeed, pushing forward in one area can lead to an explosion of challenges elsewhere. Not only might that person be a little frazzled or under pressure, but you can bet the key players at the top of any organisation are somewhat preoccupied with the organisation's future.

If you work for a firm, what are your experiences of change? How well does your organisation appear to be set up for and coping with change? In addition to exploring the impact of change closer to home, most lawyers work with a broad range of clients, perhaps in different industry sectors. This allows you to gain an invaluable 'helicopter perspective' on a range of (possibly competitor) businesses. How are those client organisations coping with change? What is different or similar about their approach to each other and the route being taken by your company?

It is interesting how some companies seem able to surf the wave of change while others struggle with a marginal difference. Many organisations are adept at organising and planning but are less prepared for taking advantage of change imposed by factors beyond their control. The reasons for this are as complicated as you can imagine and are likely to be unique for every business. How does your organisation measure up?

How likely is it that your organisational culture is mobilised for change? Speculation on the future is always risky. However, Kotter argues that "the rate of change in the business world is not going to slow down any time soon; if anything, competition in most industries will probably speed up".[5] What distinguishes readiness for change, he proposes, is the sense of urgency or complacency in an organisation. And that sense of urgency is partly fed by having access to excellent data and a culture of

5 John P Kotter, *Leading Change*, Harvard Business Review Press, 2012, p169.

open and honest communication. Kotter produced his much-admired "8-Step Process for Leading Change",[6] which advocated creating a sense of urgency; building a coalition; having a vision; enlisting support; removing barriers; generating quick wins; and sustaining and instituting success. In this, he was the first person to set out a replicable process for achieving transformative results.

Organisations that embrace change today are dominating global business (Amazon, Tesla). A crucial role of business leaders is to be aware of the change needed, have an agile concept of the organisation's future and its place globally, and develop reactions and mechanisms to address what lies ahead. To respond to these challenges and build a competitive advantage, businesses have to be extraordinarily agile and flexible. They must also hire the right people and foster cultures that encourage diversity and open questioning of norms or assumptions.

Organisations won't just change because of new systems, processes or infrastructure. They evolve because people within the organisation adapt too. Only when people have gone on their journey towards change can the organisation truly embrace and benefit from change. In Brené Brown's introduction to *Dare to Lead*,[7] she talks about brave leaders and courage cultures and that courage is a collection of four skill sets supported by 28 behaviours.

5. How can your practice thrive amidst change?

Life is a journey of learning, growth and some pain for most of us. If you want to make or accept change, you'll have to be honest with yourself. Articulating your natural point of view and concerns will help you find solutions that can lead you to action and results. It can be quite a long process, which consists of many steps. Only then can

6 John P Kotter, "The 8-Step Process for Leading Change", www.kotterinc.com/8-steps-process-for-leading-change/.

7 Brené Brown, *Dare to Lead*, Vermillion London, 2018, introduction.

you begin to design a strategy that builds on your strengths and fills in any gaps.

We recommend a regular stocktake where you explore your attitudes, identify the new skills you will need, refine existing capabilities and stop behaviours that will become surplus to requirements or even reputationally damaging.

5.1 Keep challenging yourself

Perhaps it's time to ask yourself a few uncomfortable questions. In our experience of coaching others, the more willing a person is to do this, the greater the possibility of reaching or exceeding goals. Keep asking yourself questions along the following lines until the answer becomes clear. Ponder alone or debate these with a colleague.

- Is there a need for change? If so, where? Or is there a change happening right now?
- What do I think and feel about this change?
- Do I know why this change needs to occur, or is it taking place currently?
- What do I see as my role in this change? How does it affect me and my part?
- What are the opportunities in this change?
- What are the challenges (or threats) about this change?
- What are my strengths and weaknesses concerning this change?
- What is my track record with and experience of this change?
- What do I need to do next about this change?
- Who or what can help me with this change?

5.2 The five whys

Toyota developed this approach to understanding why the business needed new product features or manufacturing techniques – asking 'why' five times is generally sufficient to arrive at the root cause of any problem.

Why?
Why?
Why?
Why?
Why?

You can even repeat the process, applying these questions to just about any change that has come onto your radar. Do you get a sense of your readiness for change from your answers? Do you have a better understanding of why you resist change and what you might need to do about it?

If you do not know how to ask the right question, you discover nothing.
W Edwards Deming[8]

There are no easy solutions. Adapt processes to suit the change intended. Change requires teamwork and leadership (and the two are related). Work with the culture (even when you want to change it). Communicate, communicate and communicate.

As John Kotter stated in the preface to his book: "Speed of change is the driving force. Leading change competitively is the only answer."[9] And change management skills are much valued in the boardroom.

They always say time changes things, but you have to change them yourself.
Andy Warhol[10]

6. Conclusion

Never confuse motion with action.
Benjamin Franklin[11]

8 William Edwards Deming (1900–1993) is widely acknowledged as the leading management thinker in the field of quality. This is a widely quoted citation and more about Deming is available here: https://deming.org/.
9 John P Kotter, *Leading Change*, Harvard Business Review Press, 2012, preface.
10 www.brainyquote.com/quotes/andy_warhol_109768.
11 www.brainyquote.com/quotes/benjamin_franklin_140816.

What are your key action points from reading this final chapter? Let's finish with 10 final coaching questions:

1. What is my attitude to change?
2. What is my level of resistance to change?
3. Do I understand why I feel this way?
4. What do I think is the source of my attitude to change?
5. Overall, how would I describe my change personality?
6. What change is most affecting my organisation (and my client organisations) currently?
7. What change(s) will impact my legal career most?
8. What specific thing(s) could I do to develop my mental resilience to change?
9. What specific thing(s) could I do to optimise my career for change?
10. What help might I need in dealing with change?

As we are at the end of the book, it's time to hand over the reins. What are the coaching questions you need to ask yourself right now based on everything you've read? Feel free to let your ideas flow.

Ultimately, riding the wave of change is about seeing opportunity in business and the legal sector and leveraging that to fulfil your potential. You may also need to learn to cope with surprise and adversity in an accepting and calm way. Be accountable to your inner change-maker, and don't be afraid to take some risks.

The future depends on what we do in the present.
Mahatma Gandhi[12]

12 www.goodreads.com/quotes/806111-the-future-depends-on-what-we-do-in-the-present.

Conclusion

Clare Jones

---

1. Where are you now?

"I want to be happier in my day-to-day work."

"I want to realise my potential."

"They're out to get me."

"I want to make more money."

"They're driving me to an early grave."

"This just isn't sustainable."

Might you say any of these? You're not alone in being dissatisfied with the status quo. Disillusionment is rife and legal careers are no different from any other role. Although many people find change difficult, most of us yearn for a more rewarding and fulfilling work experience. An average life of around 80 years is about 4,000 weeks (Office for National Statistics, National life tables – life expectancy in the UK: 2017 to 2019).[1] We spend much of our lives working. Why not make the experience simply better?

> *Lack of direction, not lack of time, is the problem. We all have twenty-four hour days.*
>
> Zig Ziglar[2]

1 www.ons.gov.uk/peoplepopulationandcommunity/birthsdeathsandmarriages/lifeexpectancies.

2 www.goodreads.com/quotes/270489-lack-of-direction-not-lack-of-time-is-the-problem.

You chose to read this book because you are thinking about your career trajectory. It might mean you want to change some aspect of your job; you might want to change your firm or even your profession. Either way, you'll need to build and flex your skill set and make it resilient for what lies ahead. We hope your head is brimming with thoughts, plans and ideas. We know you may also be thinking: 'How on earth do I begin the process of future-proofing my career?'

Before you think about the future, why not have a go at measuring where you are in your professional development right now against the 10 themes presented in our book? We don't suggest you should, or need to, get good at everything. It's about understanding who you are, where you are on your path and deciding where to put your energy going forward. Perhaps you'll highlight two or three areas you'd like to focus on. You are the master of your destiny. So take what you need and leave the rest behind.

Figure 1 is an example of a 'wheel of future skills' plotted out on a scale of 1–10. You can see the person who completed this sees themselves as a strong leader with clear goals and an ability to innovate and win work. They're not so sure about their change-readiness, ideas or ability to collaborate and build relationships. Perhaps these are areas for focus.

Figure 1: Wheel of future skills

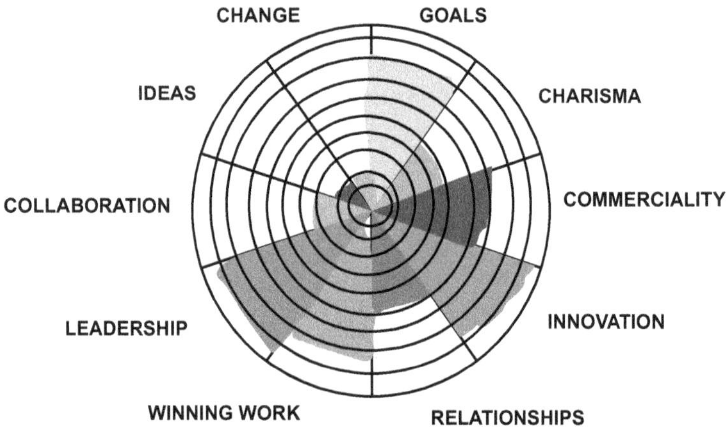

Figure 2: Blank template: Create your 'wheel of future skills'

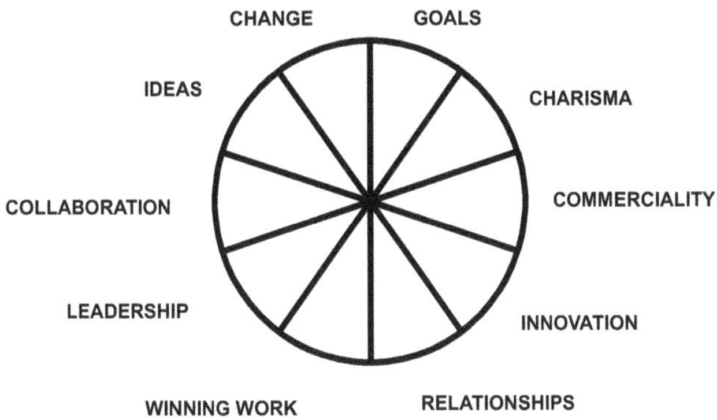

Equally, building on existing strengths could be a great strategy. Can one person be great at everything? The answer is almost certainly 'no'.

It may be helpful to visualise your 'wheel of future skills' to plot your current position. We have provided you with a blank template to do this (see Figure 2). Estimating your skills is a subjective exercise but will give you a quick summary of what you perceive as your strengths and weaknesses now and your starting point for any work you now might choose to do.

When you complete your 'wheel of future skills', we suggest you share this with a trusted 'critical friend'. What do they agree with and, perhaps, disagree with? How might they estimate your future career skills differently? Why? And what might you do next to address any areas for development?

2. What is your vision for your future career?

If you've picked this book up, browsed through it or read it cover to cover, it's a signal that your career matters to you. We believe that you must take control of your destiny as a lawyer. Throughout our book, we've presented evidence from various experts and shared experience from hundreds of coaching conversations and our other professional insights. We believe that you can coach yourself into the best possible (and most sustainable) career space for you going forward! From the first chapter to the final chapter, our book's primary message is that fate, luck and the stars may have their place, but your career happiness and future success is primarily in your hands. And we believe you can have everything you desire by building on the skills you already have. Own it. You're worth it!

Everything that you are and can be is up to you now. Good luck, and make it happen!

3. What practical steps will support your future career?

Regardless of your feelings about your current career, we've discussed a broad array of potential avenues for you to now explore, from building your charisma and upping your relationship game to becoming more commercial and innovative.

Here's some good news: you can make positive change, starting today. As helpful as it might be to have one-to-one support from a personal executive coach, it's not always feasible, and you can become clear on what you want and how to get there by coaching yourself.

All you need is an open mind, a place to record your thoughts and an hour or so alone for a truly enlightening self-coaching session using our '100 questions to ask yourself to future-proof your legal career' in Table 1, a summary of all the critical questions in this book, below. It's time to stretch yourself and leave that comfort zone. We encourage you to be honest with yourself about your weaknesses, acknowledge your strengths and be open to opportunities.

4. What's next for you?

Before we go, we want to ask you: 'What will you do now?'

Is someone who is future-proofing their career going to let this book gather dust and get back to what they have always done?

Table 1: Questions to ask yourself

Theme	*100 questions to ask yourself to future-proof your legal career*	Actions
Goals	1. Who sets my goals? 2. Is my career already mapped out for me? 3. Am I at risk of drifting? 4. What is success to me? 5. What do I see myself doing on a day-to-day basis inside my career and life? 6. How do I want to feel about the various aspects of my life (excited, energised)? 7. Do I want to spend more time doing a particular activity, or perhaps less time doing it? 8. What is my vision, and what are my goals and priorities for the next 12 months? 9. What potential obstacles do I think might be in my way? 10. What steps could I take now to bring my goals to life?	
Charisma	1. What does the word charisma mean to me? 2. Who do I know to be charismatic? 3. What attributes do they have? 4. What is it about that person or people that I admire or notice most? 5. How would I describe my charisma (in relative terms)? 6. Is my charisma natural, or have I had to work at it? 7. What is working about my charisma now, and how might I enhance that? 8. Do I think I should attempt to develop more charisma? In what way? 9. If so, what should I stop doing that is hindering my charisma? 10. How might I measure my charisma and what might I learn?	
Commerciality	1. What does commercial awareness mean to me as a lawyer, to my clients and my firm? 2. How has the meaning of commercial awareness developed as I moved from an aspiring lawyer to an experienced legal advisor?	

continued on next page

Theme	*100 questions to ask yourself to future-proof your legal career*	Actions
	3. How would I educate a new trainee or paralegal on the meaning of commercial awareness if they were working with me? 4. How would I encourage them to develop their sense of commercial awareness? 5. Who are my most long-standing clients? 6. In terms of commerciality, who are my most profitable clients? 7. How has my commercial awareness of these clients' businesses and personalities aided me in retaining them? 8. How has my commercial awareness of these clients' businesses and personalities aided me in developing that relationship? 9. What more could I learn about them? 10. What further questions could I ask to demonstrate my interest in my clients' way of doing business?	
Innovation	1. Where have I seen examples of successful innovation (inside and outside the law)? 2. What can I learn from the best examples of innovation? 3. Where have I noticed attempts at innovation which have not proven successful? 4. Why do I think these attempts failed? 5. What are the lessons from these examples? 6. When I consider my favourite brands or service providers I use regularly, what is it about their service that I really like? 7. What can I learn from these examples? 8. As I consider my role/department/team right now, what opportunities for innovation do I see? 9. Where is time being wasted, or perhaps tasks being replicated? 10. What could be made more efficient in terms of time, money or people power?	

continued on next page

Theme	*100 questions to ask yourself to future-proof your legal career*	Actions
Relationships	1. How can I build a stronger client portfolio that anticipates future needs? 2. To what extent am I working from a fixed mindset rather than a growth mindset? 3. What changes should I plan to my working practices to achieve more of what will motivate me in five years' time? 4. What am I assuming about my client that may no longer be valid? 5. What are the best questions that I can ask my client to increase my awareness of their perspective and our working relationship? 6. How do I demonstrate to each of my clients that I am adapting to meet their individual and organisational needs? 7. Who are the three people most critical for my business with this client that I do not know yet? 8. What can my organisation do that my client is unaware of? 9. What needs are my competitors seeing in my clients that I have yet to notice? 10. What do I do that keeps my competitors awake at night?	
Winning work	1. What am I doing on a daily basis to build my network? 2. What is the first thing I need to do to improve my sales hustle? 3. How can I better communicate with prospects in future? 4. How do I ensure I qualify opportunities and not waste effort with the wrong prospects in the longer term? 5. How am I ensuring I have a competitive value proposition? 6. What is my pricing strategy? 7. What systems and processes do I have to help me to win work? 8. How could I improve these to help me to win work?	

continued on next page

Theme	*100 questions to ask yourself to future-proof your legal career*	Actions
	9. What can I do to better learn from pitches I win and lose? 10. What do I need to do to ensure I keep my clients and gain referrals?	
Leadership	1. How do I adapt my leadership approach to match changing circumstances appropriately? 2. As a leader, how often do I praise my colleagues' strengths? 3. Who can I ask to compensate for my leadership weaknesses? 4. How do I continuously create the space needed to avoid cognitive overload? 5. Why should I lead anyone? 6. What do I do regularly to demonstrate my trust in those around me? 7. What are the limiting factors of my leadership that I have not addressed? 8. What previous strengths have I stopped deploying regularly and why? 9. To what extent am I not using the potential of my brain? 10. In the next 12 months, how will I adapt my leadership approach to meet changing VUCA needs?	
Collaboration	1. How can I build greater trust and collaborate more effectively with others? 2. What behaviours are most valuable for me when I am working in teams? 3. How can I make it more attractive for other practice areas to collaborate with my service area? 4. How open am I and this team to the creativity that co-opting a 'rebel' could bring to our thinking? 5. What would allow me to contribute more to this team? 6. To what extent would my team's performance improve if I spent time away from my instinctive approach? 7. How consciously do I adapt my approach to work with colleagues from different cultural backgrounds? 8. Why am I feeling the way I feel about my colleague?	

continued on next page

Theme	*100 questions to ask yourself to future-proof your legal career*	Actions
	9. Stakeholders frequently complain about not hearing enough from teams. How do my teams choose the appropriate level of connection for each part of the system? 10. Regarding the Agile Manifesto, which preferences for better ways of working are appropriate for my teams and me?	
Ideas	1. What is my understanding of thought leadership? 2. Do I want to be a thought leader? 3. Who is my ideal audience for my ideas? 4. What does my audience want most from me? 5. How can I best articulate my unique point of view? 6. Which are my best channels (for example, blogs, case studies, reports, articles, books, speaking, podcasting, social media, webinars, infographics, etc)? 7. What are the first steps I need to take to bring my ideas to my audience? 8. How will I measure the benefit of my efforts to build my reputation? 9. How will I protect my reputation and manage any reputational risks? 10. What help can I get to produce and hone my content?	
Change	1. What is my attitude to change? 2. What is my level of resistance to change? 3. Do I understand why I feel this way? 4. What do I think is the source of my attitude to change? 5. Overall, how would I describe my change personality? 6. What change is most affecting my organisation (and my client organisations) currently? 7. What change(s) will impact my legal career most? 8. What specific thing(s) could I do to develop my mental resilience to change? 9. What specific thing(s) could I do to optimise my career for change? 10. What help might I need in dealing with change?	

We would love that you might get out your highlighter pen or create some notes; we want you to metaphorically dog-ear the pages of this book that resonate most with you and make an action list. We'd be thrilled to know that you might share your thoughts on your future career whilst inspiring a colleague or friend with your new wisdom and getting them into a positive mindset whilst reinforcing your learning.

Above all, we want you to take action. We want you to do something different. Now is not the time to play safe. It's time to reimagine your career and engage with the excitement of change and all the possibilities that it brings.

It would be great to hear from you if you have any questions or comments or you'd like support with future-proofing your career. We'd love to hear your story and understand your journey. Do contact any of us: Clare Jones (Clare.Jones@TLTsolicitors.com), Steve Couch (steve@coachingtogether.co.uk) and Hannah Beko (hannah@authenticallyspeaking.co.uk).

Also, visit www.futureproofyourlegalcareer.com for tools, tips and resources.

About the authors

Clare Jones
Chief marketing officer, TLT LLP
Clare.Jones@TLTsolicitors.com

Clare Jones is chief marketing officer at TLT LLP, a top 50 UK law firm, and is a chartered marketer with a master's degree in coaching from the University of Warwick. In her 25-year career she has led business development and marketing functions within a range of international professional service firms. In digital agency roles, she has helped create exciting campaigns, products and platforms.

As a consultant, coach and trainer, she has advised firms on strategy and change. She has also helped hundreds of individual lawyers to develop their skills such as building their personal brands, winning work and managing clients.

Steve Couch
Managing director, Coaching Together Ltd
steve@coachingtogether.co.uk

As the managing director of Coaching Together Ltd, Steve Couch works with senior executives and leadership teams as a business coach. Many of his clients are individual partners and senior teams in professional services organisations. Steve is also an experienced presenter, and designer of business development events and conferences.

Steve's approach reflects more than 30 years' experience of providing advice to multinational clients, and, more recently, extensive study and research.

As a PwC partner, Steve led large, successful practices based in the UK, the Netherlands, and across Central and Eastern Europe. After leaving PwC, Steve moved into coaching practice and spent three years working towards a Masters in Coaching & Behavioural Change (with distinction). His research on the behaviours of culturally different members of international business teams, was published by the British Psychological Society in 2020.

Steve closely follows Premiership Rugby and is a keen skier.

Hannah Beko
Lawyer, coach and trainer, Authentically Speaking
hannah@authenticallyspeaking.co.uk

Hannah Beko is a highly knowledgeable, personable and practical commercial property lawyer. Having worked as a self-employed consultant since 2012 she works with investors, developers and occupiers on acquisitions and disposals, financing, development, corporate and insolvency support, providing training and support to investors in relation to the more creative property strategies.

Alongside her legal business and young family, Hannah founded her coaching and training consultancy Authentically Speaking in 2016 and works within the legal profession to encourage the improvement of key skills such as stress management, improving emotional well-being, confidence and performance, career decision making and becoming more authentic lawyers.

Hannah is also a podcast host and the author of *The Authentic Lawyer*. She is passionate about bringing about change to the culture and practice of law.

Index

About Globe Law and Business

Globe Law and Business was established in 2005. From the very beginning, we set out to create law books which are sufficiently high level to be of real use to the experienced professional, yet still accessible and easy to navigate. Most of our authors are drawn from Magic Circle and other top commercial firms, both in the UK and internationally.

Our titles are carefully produced, with the utmost attention paid to editorial, design and production processes. We hope this results in high-quality publications that are easy to read, and a pleasure to own. Our titles are also available as ebooks, which are compatible with most desktop, laptop and tablet devices. In 2018 we expanded our portfolio to include journals and Special Reports, available both digitally and in hard copy format, and produced to the same high standards as our books.

In the Spring of 2021, we were very pleased to announce the start of a new chapter for Globe Law and Business following the acquisition of law books under the imprint Ark Publishing. We are very much looking forward to working with our new Ark authors, many of whom are well-known to us, and to further developing the law firm management list, among other areas.

We'd very much like to hear from you with your thoughts and ideas for improving what we offer. Please do feel free to email me at sian@globelawandbusiness.com with your views.

Sian O'Neill
Managing director
Globe Law and Business
www.globelawandbusiness.com

www.ingramcontent.com/pod-product-compliance
Ingram Content Group UK Ltd.
Pitfield, Milton Keynes, MK11 3LW, UK
UKHW050023141125
465057UK00003B/12

9 781787 424265